Seeds in the Wind

Survival and Freedom From Trafficking, Slavery and Exploitation

A Novel by

Ed Schwartz

First Edition - 2021

OAK CREEK
media

Bluffton, Indiana

First Editor Copyright – 2021
by Ed Schwartz

ISBN: 978-1-7336505-6-4

Copyrighted Material

Dedication

THOUSANDS of girls and women walk the night-time streets of Addis Ababa, Ethiopia selling the only thing they have to offer. Few have made a willing choice to give up their independence and dignity, but rather have been exploited and trafficked into hopeless tragedy. They along with their children are stuck in a cycle of poverty and hopelessness we can only imagine.

I pray that 'Seeds in the Wind' will give them and their children a voice that leads to advocacy and assistance helping them achieve their God-given potential.

This book is dedicated to girls and women around the world suffering from trafficking, exploitation and abuse. I've met many of these girls and women and heard their heart-wrenching stories but have chosen these two young girls to highlight the thousands and thousands of others.

The first is a fifteen-year-old girl in Addis Ababa who had been on the streets for three years when I met her.

The second girl is seventeen-years-old and seven months pregnant. She said she'd be working on the streets until the day she would gave birth.

Secondly, we dedicate this book to the many organizations and individuals committed to serving the last, lost, least and lonely of the world.

Introduction

ONE of the most difficult things to read about are the sad tragedies happening to common, good and innocent people. Our minds are repulsed by the evil inflicted upon some human beings by others. We tend to push away the harsh realities affecting many people around the world. Yet, we do need to know. Or, sadly, things stay the same.

This novel, *Seeds in the Wind*, is about six young girls from Ethiopia (Mariam, Zoya, Makda, Lola, Maya and Hana) and how their lives become intertwined. Each are enmeshed in their very personal tragedy of human trafficking and exploitation. Whether it occurs within a country or across international borders, the results tend to be the same.

The heartbreak of trafficking and exploitation unfolds in nearly every country around the world. I've seen the devastating effects in the U.S.A., Haiti, Ethiopia and India over the last thirty-five years and sadly, I realize I've only seen the tip of a massive iceberg.

Personally witnessing the results of many tragic stories has culminated in a series of novels regarding the darkness and horror of slavery, trafficking and exploitation.

It's my hope that *Seeds in the Wind*, along with the first three books in my *Trufficking* series - *The Trade Winds*; *A Rose Among Thorns*; and *Esther's Legacy* - will shine a revealing spotlight on the tragedy that besets so many of the last, lost, least and lonely among us.

This novel seeks to highlight how God is able, in His redeeming fashion, to bring good from bad anytime and anywhere. His Gospel message of salvation isn't deterred by greed, wickedness, governments or international borders. Just as seeds from a plant are carried by the wind, so is His Good News traversing the globe.

PART 1

- Life at Home -

Week 1

August 30 – September 6, 2015

Chapter 1

Central Bus Station – Addis Ababa, Ethiopia
4:15 p.m. – Tuesday, September 1, 2015

MARIAM

SHE cowered in the dark shadows of the chilly late afternoon. Overcome with numbing fear, her small hands trembled and her heart raced. Subconsciously she put her hand on her chest in a hopeless effort to calm the pounding.

The bald-headed man who brought her to the bus station was undoubtedly and frantically searching for her. But she knew an impatient and desperate peek at the crowd could reveal her location.

Sitting in the wet dirt behind a meat vendor's stall, Mariam pushed herself tighter against the wood slatted wall. She quickly recoiled as a rust encrusted nail protruding from a slat punctured her shoulder. She winced but didn't cry out.

The chilly dampness of the ground was penetrating her bones and her shivering became worse, but she knew she had to remain still. Noticing blood on her hand, she looked at her shoulder to see how badly the nail had injured her. She saw a round mark, but there was no blood. Looking at her hand again, she wondered where all the blood was coming from.

Her senses reacted as she realized the wet ground she was sitting on was saturated in blood. Then she understood. This was a meat vendor's stall and butchering was likely done right where she was sitting. Suddenly the smell of her hiding place began to permeate her senses. She'd been so intent on escaping from Baldy she hadn't noticed the smell and slime of the ground she sat on. She shifted but the move only made matters worse as the smell was stirred once again. The blood invaded yet more dry spots of her clothing and body. She suppressed a gag.

To calm herself, she began thinking about her father. As Muslim's, they had practiced the Quran's teaching on *halāl* foods that were lawful to eat and the unlawful *harām* foods which weren't. She'd been taught it was unlawful to consume blood, meat from a pig, or any meat from an animal that had died naturally. She wondered if it was okay to be sitting in blood or to have blood on your hands. She made a mental note not to touch her face with her hands. At nine years old, Mariam knew she had a lot to learn from the Quran.

Her mind was quickly jolted back to reality as she heard shouting on the other side of her hide-out. She wondered if it was Baldy creating a commotion. She knew he'd been incredibly angry when she'd slipped away from him. Then the ruckus died down almost as quickly as it had started.

The smell of the hanging meat, the blood saturated dirt and whatever else was scattered around brought on another unacceptable gag. Two dogs stopped to sniff the ground nearby but didn't pay any attention to her. They hungrily devoured a pile of slimy entrails only ten feet away from her. Mariam settled in, hoping she could endure the slow-moving two hours before nightfall.

The main bus station in central Addis Ababa was an incredibly busy place. With colorful buses arriving at all hours of the day and night from all over the country, there was never a quiet time or absence of people. The poor from the remote country regions ignorantly considered the capital city of Addis Ababa to be a paradise and a city of countless jobs.

Desperately trying to shut out the terror of being found, as well as seeking to dampen the noises and smells surrounding her, she permitted her mind to wander, which quickly took her to recent memories of her family.

It had only been three days since she'd been surrounded by those she loved and those who loved her. Yet, those three days had slowly drug on and on. She visualized her mother's face and realized she almost always had a smile. Her eyes radiated warmth and love.

Tears came as she realized how much she missed her family. At nine-years-old, she was the oldest of four children. The youngest was a six month old baby girl named Neela whom she adored. Mariam had become Neela's personal caretaker from birth and there was no doubt in her mind that caring for her baby sister was the best part of her life.

Growing up in a remote part of Ethiopia, she'd only known dry, hot and arid desert life. Their life was simple and focused on finding enough food and water to survive.

Her father had once told her of an African proverb from the Tuareg tribe in the Saharan Desert – *'God created lands with lakes and rivers for people to live, but he created the desert so a man can find his soul'*. Mariam didn't know exactly what the proverb meant, but she knew her father was encouraging her to enjoy the life Allah had given them.

There had been no extra income for unnecessary things or luxuries in their lives, so her family was fanatically devoted to one another. There was however, a small goatskin bag she periodically opened to see how much money her father had. The amount would ebb and flow and she quietly wondered what would happen if he was unable to work. Looking in the bag and seeing the coins and currency had given her a degree of security. He hid the bag in a small cabinet where her mother kept their precious dishes. Mariam smiled as she recalled her favorite plate which had multiple cracks in it. The cracks resembled a three-legged camel.

Her father had been fortunate to get a job working at a local farm. The farmer who employed him had many acres of peppers, tomatoes and carrots next to a large river. The farmer also grew maize and sorghum and used channels of water to irrigate the fields. Mariam's father was kept busy digging channels and working in the fields. Along with the money he received, they felt blessed as a family to have plenty of fruit, vegetables and corn meal from the farmer.

Others in the area weren't as fortunate. When a drought came, famine would rapidly follow and then everyone suffered.

It was nearly impossible to keep their home clean in the dusty and dry desert. Their round home with a thatched roof was constructed from twigs, straw and mud. Along with her family, the tukul was home to two cows, three goats, nine chickens and a donkey. Though the livestock was outside during most of the day, they sheltered inside the home during the hottest time of day and during the night.

Her father had often told her the history of the long disputed border between Somalia and Ethiopia. He said civil wars and border disputes since the 1970's had been a big part of his life. The land they now lived on was just sixty miles from the border and had once been part of Somalia. Then war moved the border east. Now they were proud Somalians living in Ethiopia.

Right now she wasn't feeling very proud. Her white 'guntiino' was incredibly dirty. The long, wide strip of fabric wrapped around her shoulders and waist. The traditional dress was now stained horribly. The red and black decorative trim on the edges now matched the stains from the meat vendor's dirt.

She remembered the day, just three days ago, when she'd walked to the river...

It had been another hot day and she dreaded the ten minute walk to the river, but the twenty minute walk back carrying the four gourds of water was always the hardest part.

Arriving at the river, she noticed she was alone, so she stepped to the edge of the water. Undressing, she jumped in the cool water and was so glad for the refreshing break from the desert heat.

Ten minutes later she saw a bald-headed man standing on the bank of the river by her small pile of clothing. He waved at her and then went up the bank and disappeared. Waiting a couple of minutes she quickly emerged and dressed. She began filling the first gourd with water when the man reappeared and came toward her.

He grabbed her small arm and pulled her up the bank. She screamed again and again but knew no one was near enough to hear her desperate cries. Glancing back she saw her gourds lying on the bank next to the river.

Stumbling behind the man, she fell. He pulled Mariam to her feet and pulled her toward a white truck. Opening the door he roughly pushed her inside and went around the truck and got into the driver's seat.

Desperate and trembling, she looked at the stranger and whispered, "What are you doing?"

He merely looked at her as the truck sped along the dusty desert road. In the distance she could barely see the branches, stuck in the ground, which created the fence around her home. The truck raced on, into the desert.

She'd begun to cry. The man quickly swung his right hand and slapped her on the face. He glared at her and said, "Baby girl, you belong to me now. There's nothing you can do to get away and you'd better understand that. I promise you, if you whimper, cry or try to get help from anyone in the next few days, you'll regret it. That slap was nothing compared to what'll happen to you the next time!"

He continued driving north along the river. An hour later they arrived in Gode. Mariam had only been to the large city one other time with her father. She'd been amazed at the size of the city and the massive amounts of people.

She remembered asking her father, "How many people live here?"

"More than a million!"

"A million? How many is that?"

Her father had smiled and said, "If you began counting all the hairs on our two cows, three goats, donkey and on our family's heads, you might get to a million."

It was strange she'd never known the name of the city. Suddenly her thoughts were interrupted by 'Baldy'. "What are you smiling at?"

She said nothing.

Again, "What are you smiling at?"

"I was just thinking about my father."

Baldy replied, "I don't want to hurt you, but I will if I have to. I just have a job to do. In Addis Ababa, where we'll be in a few days, I'm delivering you to someone who will find you a job. There are a lot of wealthy families in Addis who need help caring for their house and kids. I keep busy finding girls in the country-side to work for those families."

It almost seemed like he was apologetic as he continued, "I've seen how families in the desert country struggle. They have a hard life with little water, no fertile ground and not enough food to eat. Where I'm taking you, you'll have everything you need. Someday, you'll thank me for rescuing you from all of that."

Mariam silently thought, 'You have no idea how good my family life is'.

"We're going to stop and get something to eat, then we'll get on a bus to go to Addis."

Baldy threaded his way through the streets of Gode and then maneuvered his truck into a large parking lot. Looking at Mariam he said, "Young'un, this is another warning. I don't want you crying, asking someone for help and even looking like you're in trouble... or believe me, you'll be in big trouble!

"I'm going to get you cleaned up and then we'll get something to eat. The bus will be leaving in two hours. It's a lot cheaper for us to take the bus than for me to drive the 700 miles to Addis. So, get out of the truck and treat me like I'm your papa and we'll get along just fine."

Mariam opened the door and stepped down. Baldy came around the truck and gave her a bottle of water and cloth rag. "Here, clean yourself. You might be from the country, but you can't look like this."

A few minutes later, he reached down and grabbed her hand as together they walked toward a food stand.

He ordered for both of them and soon they were sitting on the ground under a nearby tree.

The injera flat bread and vegetable curry didn't taste like her mothers, but it was good and too quickly gone.

They walked to the bus station where Baldy purchased two tickets for the ride to Addis. Walking to the bus, he said, "Stay close to me. I'll get us a seat. It's going to get crowded and not everyone will have a place to sit."

Mariam watched Baldy maneuver his way through the many people, using his elbows to carefully work his way to the front of the crowd. He was successful in getting on the bus with Mariam in tow.

Sitting down in a seat by a window, she watched her fellow-passengers coming on board. There were all shapes and sizes, varying complexions, decorations, jewelry and hair styles, all of which expanded her small world. The seats were filled. A number of people were left standing in the aisle.

She hadn't realized how different she looked from other Ethiopians until she got on the large bus and watched as other passengers got on. Most of the people had much lighter skin than her own. Her father had told her they were of the Ogaden clan of Somalia and she should always be proud of her darker skin and heritage.

The door closed and the bus lurched forward causing those in the aisle to quickly grab the overhead handles.

Mariam's journey to Addis had begun.

Over the next two days, she watched as the countryside went from brown to green. Passengers exited the bus and made room for more.

The temptation to escape had been strong but the opportunities were not readily available because Baldy kept her by the window. She would have had to crawl over him to escape and she knew that wasn't going to happen.

The bus arrived in Addis at noon. They stopped at two small bus stations where again, passengers got off and on. Then, mid-afternoon, the bus pulled into a large station. There were dozens of buses and hundreds of people. It was like a small city inside a much larger city.

Baldy patiently waited for the crowded bus to empty the human cargo, then stood up, grabbing Mariam's hand. Emerging from the empty bus, she stepped down onto a muddy street. Looking around, she was amazed at the chaos created by all the cars, bicycles, vendors and people. Mariam tugged at her guntiino to keep it from dragging in the puddles of water and mud.

It was at that moment, a moving bicyclist, ten feet away grabbed a woman's bag from her hand and veered into the street for his getaway. The woman fell onto the street and cursed. A car swerved to miss the bicycle and veered toward Baldy and Mariam. He dropped her hand as the car narrowly missed him. The car's front tire dropped into a rain-filled pothole and splattered him.

Baldy was irate as he concentrated on the driver of the car. While he was screaming curses and shaking his fist, Mariam saw her chance. She simply backed up and was swallowed by the crowd of people going about their business.

Quickly, she ducked behind the line of vendor's booths. Then she ran. Finally, she stopped, out of breath in front of a meat vendor's booth. She quickly disappeared behind it and hid.

Thinking about her distant family and her now dangerous situation, caused her to wonder what to do next. How could she get home? She didn't have money for a bus ticket. She was hungry, cold, tired, and certainly very afraid.

The dogs had moved on, though the wet earth and smells from the blood and meat were still present. Darkness was approaching and the street lights around the bus station had come on. She guessed she'd been hiding in this spot for over two hours.

Then, a woman came around the corner of the booth and smiled at her. Mariam pushed tighter against the slats but the woman approached her. Squatting down, the woman gave her a slice of bread and smiled. She said, "Stay quiet, you'll be okay."

The woman disappeared as quickly as she'd come.

Quietly and with appreciation Mariam began eating the bread.

Two minutes later, the woman reappeared and Baldy was with her. He quickly grabbed Mariam's arm and held it angrily. With his free hand he reached into his pocket and placed some coins in the woman's outstretched hand. She quickly left.

Baldy slapped Mariam twice. He grimaced as he smelled the stench of rotting meat and blood. Looking at her dress, he slapped her again and said, "Now you'll have to get cleaned up and I'll need to find a new guntiino for you to wear."

His face was contorted with anger as he pulled her beside him and they walked down the street.

He found a vendor selling cloth and purchased the white material for Mariam.

It was obvious Baldy knew his way around the bus station as he headed directly to a public bathroom. He said, "There's only one way in and one way out, so get in there and get cleaned up."

Handing her the guntiino, he continued, "And put this on and throw your old one away."

Cowering, Mariam went inside.

Soon, she emerged, scared, but looking clean and fresh.

"That's better."

Looking around, he began walking, tugging Mariam alongside him. In five minutes he approached a taxi and they got in. The taxi moved into traffic. Mariam was amazed at the size of Addis. She thought the city where they got on the bus was huge, but this was much larger.

She watched as brightly lit stores and businesses flashed by. People were everywhere.

Twenty minutes later the taxi stopped in front of a tall stone wall. Baldy said, "Get out. We've arrived."

After paying the driver, they walked to a bright blue, steel door inset in the stone wall. Baldy knocked and immediately a guard opened the door and let them inside. The two men knew each other and talked briefly. Baldy and Mariam stood quietly as the guard entered the front door of a huge home.

Soon, he returned and invited them to sit on the veranda of the home's courtyard. A woman in a white dress brought a tray of small cakes and iced drinks.

Baldy, without emotion, motioned to Mariam and said, "Go ahead and eat."

She reluctantly took a small cake, looked at it and hesitantly nibbled the edge. It was sweet, soft and even warm. The small nibbles became bites as it quickly disappeared. She took another cake. The drink was equally sweet and tasted like some kind of fruit.

Looking around the courtyard she couldn't believe how beautiful it was. There were trees, shrubs and flowers everywhere. In the desert there was very little color other than the normal shades of brown and tan. She'd never seen such beauty and wondered what the inside of the house was like.

Abruptly a middle-aged woman came through the front door to the veranda.

"Tebeb! It's so good to see you. Have you had a difficult trip?"

Without smiling, he looked at Mariam and said, "The trip had its troubles but we're here."

"So, introduce me to our guest!"

"Oh, this is Mariam. She's from the south, nine years old, strong and healthy. But she's missing her family."

Subira looked at her, smiled and said, "Mariam, my name is Subira. Don't worry, you're in a good place. I'll explain a few things to you and then we'll get you settled in your room."

Looking at Baldy she said, "Tebeb, see my secretary before you leave. She'll take care of what I owe you. As always, thanks for bringing Mariam to me. Keep in touch."

They watched as he disappeared into another room.

Subira reached out and held Mariam's hand and said, "Mariam, you've been through a lot, I'm sure, so let me explain a few things to you. First of all, I want you to know I grew up in the country. It was north of here but life was very difficult. My family rarely had enough to eat and I was unable to go to school.

"I was given the opportunity to come to Addis Ababa to work and it was the best thing that ever happened to me. The hardest part was leaving my family. Soon, I found out that with my work I was able to send them money to help them out. What started out as difficult soon turned into a blessing. I'm sure you'll see it the same way.

"I've decided to live my life in a way where I can help young girls like you have a better life. In about two weeks I'll find a family for you to live with. You can help them with the house work and their children. I'm sure you'll like it. It's a real opportunity."

Mariam said, "But Baldy... I mean Tebeb... took me away from my family. I didn't want to leave them. I have a great mother and father. Tebeb forced me to come and he wasn't very nice about it."

Subira frowned and said, "Unfortunately, sometimes that's how it begins. But, you'll see this is best. If Tebeb had simply asked you to come, would you have?"

"No, of course not."

"Well, I hope you can begin to trust me. I know what's best and I know the wonderful life you have waiting for you. I'm like a fortune teller because I know the future and all you know is the past. You'll see, this is a blessing. Now let's go inside."

Walking through the front door, Mariam had never seen such beauty. The home was brilliantly lit and white. Furniture was everywhere. There were pictures on the walls and magnificent vases on the elegantly tiled floor. There was a staircase going to a second floor. The woodwork throughout the home was a rich and deeply polished mahogany.

Subira took Mariam into the kitchen and explained how the stove, oven, refrigerator and freezer operated. Opening the cupboards, she showed her the many dishes, pots and pans. Mariam held a dish in her hands and marveled at the intricately colored floral design on the china. She was amazed there were no cracks.

Subira opened another door to reveal a stocked pantry of cans, jars and bags of food products. Mariam's jaw literally dropped.

A quick tour of the bathroom was next. Then they ascended the wide staircase to the upper level. On this floor there were multiple bedrooms, a bathroom with a shower and a large area with furniture.

Subira opened the door to a small bedroom and said, "This is your home for the next couple of weeks until we get you to your new family. If there's anything you need, let one of the maids know. I'm expecting more girls this week, so you'll soon have company. The first girl will be arriving in the morning. For tonight, try to be quiet since there's another girl named Eshe sleeping in the next room who'll be leaving in the morning. You might be able to meet her at breakfast before she leaves.

"I'm sure you're tired, so please take a shower and go to bed. Breakfast will be downstairs at eight o'clock. Sleep well."

Mariam sat on the bed. Her mind was swirling with all kinds of thoughts! How was she to make sense of all she'd been through and all she'd seen? Was this heaven on earth? Was Subira who she seemed to be? Was she to feel good about being away from her family?

Then she thought about her baby sister Neela. Mariam buried her face in the soft pillow and quietly cried. She knew this place in Addis Ababa was not where Allah wanted her to be. In spite of the beauty and luxury, her heart was drawn to her family's tukul with its familiar smells. She knew she'd give anything to have her little sister Neela in her arms once again.

Chapter 2

Adama, Ethiopia
7:00 a.m. – Tuesday, September 1, 2015

ZOYA

"YOU'D better hurry Zoya, or you'll be late for school!"

"Mom, I'm coming, I'm coming."

Sixteen-year-old Zoya had just started her second year of high school in Adama. Living on the southernmost side of the large Ethiopian city, she was more of a country girl than a city girl. Consequently, their location created a daily commute to the city high school which required more time, effort and expense than her friends had to exert.

Zoya's mom and dad were willing to sacrifice to give Zoya a better life than they'd had. Though the family was doing okay, they were certainly the lower class.

"He's here and waiting outside the gate!"

"Bye Mom. Love you. I'll be home a little late this afternoon. I'm meeting my friends at the café after school."

"You'll be with them at school, why do you need to go to the café?"

With a smile, Zoya said, "Mom, I think you were young once. I know you know the answer to that question!"

Marjani smiled as she watched her only child getting on the back of their neighbor's motorcycle. He worked in the city and they'd offered him a few birr to take Zoya to school each day.

As she washed the breakfast dishes, her mind wondered. Her husband Kojo worked hard at the large scoria quarry on the west side of Adama. They mined a special product for fortifying cement. He'd worked there for years which provided a steady income for his small family.

Lately she'd been mildly concerned with Zoya's restlessness. Was it merely a normal part of being sixteen? Maybe it was related to being in high school and the typical exposure to pressures which she herself had never experienced. She'd shared her concern with Zoya but was quickly reassured everything was going well and there wasn't anything to worry about. Zoya had said, "Mom, since you didn't go to high school, you don't know what it's like."

Then she'd said something that had hurt Marjani. "Since we live where we live, some of my classmates don't accept me. You have to have the right clothing and shoes to fit in. To them I'm just a poor girl trying to be like them."

Marjani couldn't relate as she grew up in a different era and place. She'd never bothered to tell Kojo about her conversation with Zoya. She knew it would have hurt him to know he wasn't providing well enough for his beautiful and only child. Often he'd call her 'Angel' and Marjani knew how much they loved each other.

As she finished the dishes, she couldn't quite shake the dark mood she'd allowed herself to fall into. She comforted herself quickly with the thought that she was just another mother dealing with the usual issues surrounding every teenager in Ethiopia.

After their classes, Zoya stood outside the school looking for her three friends and didn't have to wait long until they arrived. Anika, with an animated smile said, "Zoya, you're one of the prettiest girls in our entire school. I can't believe you're waiting on us instead of one of the guys!"

"Stop it. That's the funniest thing I've heard all day."

"That's one of the reasons you're so beautiful. You don't even know you are."

"What?"

"Oh, never mind. You're clueless. Let's go."

After ten minutes of walking and chatter they arrived at the Buna Tetu Café. Going inside they ordered their drinks and sat down in a booth.

Dani said, "How can it be we're all such good friends when we're all so different. Anika is Muslim, I'm Ethiopian Orthodox, Zoya is Protestant Christian and Behati is Catholic. We shouldn't even be talking together besides being best of friends!"

She continued, "Maybe the four of us should teach a class on *'Diversities of Religion!'*"

Zoya said, "My dad told me politics and religion cause most wars. He also said religion causes most divorces in families."

As the only Muslim in the small group, Anika said, "I hope we can stay best friends until we're all old women! At least I'll be able to cover my grey hairs with my *hijab*!"

The girls laughed loud enough to get some casual looks from the other customers. No one was bothered by the girls enjoying themselves. Drinking coffee together was more about relationships than about coffee. No one would dare drink alone as that would indicate they had no friends in which to confide.

Behati said, "I got a phone call last night from a cousin in Addis Ababa."

"Is she someone we know?"

"No, she's from Dire Dawa. Our mothers are sisters. Anyway, she moved to Addis to get work. She called me and said there was an opening for me if I wanted to join her. She begged me to come!"

Anika asked, "What kind of work is she doing?"

"She'll be a model for advertising. Businesses are growing quickly in Addis and they need girls for their videos and photography."

Anika looked at Zoya and said, "Remember what I said when we came out of school this afternoon?"

"No. What?"

"I said you were the most beautiful girl in the school." Then she continued, "Maybe you could become a model?"

"Well, I do remember you saying something about it. But if I remember right, you said I was *'one of the prettiest girls'*, now you said *'the most beautiful girl'*. It sounds like I can't believe anything you're saying."

The girls laughed.

Zoya looked at Behati and asked, "So, what are you going to do? Are you thinking about joining her in Addis?"

"No, I couldn't do that. Actually I don't need to work. My father's an attorney so money isn't a problem."

With their coffees finished, they walked to the front door. Hugging one another, they moved onto the sidewalk in front of the café.

As Zoya began walking toward a taxi, Behati joined her. Zoya stopped and said, "Behati, why don't you want to join your cousin? It sounds like a great opportunity."

"It's not for me. I'm settled here and I'm content. I guess I have more reasons to stay than I have to leave. I suppose if my family needed more income I'd consider it, but that's not an issue."

Zoya looked down at the sidewalk and said, "When Dani talked about all of us being so different she was right. But in one way, the three of you are alike and I'm the one who's different. Money isn't an issue for Dani, Anika or you. My family struggles and my dad has to work a lot of hours just so I can stay in school. My mom takes in laundry to wash for our neighbors. She sells vegetables at the market. I know I'm a burden for them and I feel guilty using their hard earned money so I can become a success. I'm different than the three of you."

Behati hugged her and said, "You might be the poorest of the four of us, but you have qualities that make me jealous. You're beautiful inside and out. Everyone loves your smile and we all know how sweet you are. One of the best things about you is that you're the only one who doesn't know how special you are. You're truly humble. I love that." Pausing, she continued, "Probably the most important thing is

I wish I had a relationship with my mom and dad like you have. You've got so much."

"But the things I get from them are at their expense. I see them getting old, right before my eyes, and I don't like that. I wish there was something I could do to help them."

Looking at Behati, she asked, "Would you give me the phone number for the modeling work in Addis?"

Behati looked at Zoya, then said, "I don't know. What would your mom and dad say? You'd quit school and move? I'm not sure I'd want to lose a friend like you."

Zoya said, "I'd just make a phone call to get more information. It'd be interesting to see how much money a year of modeling could bring to my family. I'm guessing it'd be quite a bit."

Then Zoya asked again, "Could I have the number?"

Hesitating, Behati said, "Only if you promise to just get information and not commit to going until you talk to me first! Okay?"

Smiling, Zoya said, "Okay. I promise."

Opening her backpack, Behati retrieved a small piece of paper and handed it to Zoya. "Let me know what they say!"

Zoya hugged her again and got into the taxi.

That evening, Zoya joined her mom and dad for supper.

"Hey Angel, how did school go today?"

Zoya looked at her dad with a smile and said, "Oh, the usual. I wish I was as smart as my friends. I have to study harder than they do. It seems to come much easier for them, especially Dani. I'm guessing she'll be a professor some day!"

"Ah, my Angel. God gave you 'beauty' and then He looked at you and said, 'This one is finished and perfect. She doesn't need anything else'!"

Zoya replied, "Papa, you know how to make me feel good. But, you know as well as I do, beauty goes away with age." Then, quickly looking at her mom, she continued with a smile, "Except for Mom. She kept her beauty."

Her mom lowered her eyes and smiled as Kojo reached up and cupped his wife's chin in his rough and worn hand. "You're right, Mom's still got her gorgeous good looks."

Marjani said, "Finish your food and quit talking crazy talk."

In the morning, Marjani said, "Zoya, you're up and ready early?"

"Yes, I need to get to school earlier today. Jemal said he'd be here with his motorcycle early, so I have to go. Love you, Mom."

As Jemal wove his way through the streets of Adama, Zoya rehearsed the upcoming phone call over and over. She was apprehensive. What would happen if the phone call went in a good direction?

Was she ready to drop out of school?

Would she need her mom's and dad's blessings to go to Addis?

Would her friendship with Behati, Dani and Anika change?

Though apprehensive, Zoya was also excited for the opportunity. But, more than anything, she wanted to contribute to her family's welfare.

Jemal stopped in front of the school and Zoya got off his motorcycle with a smile and hastily muttered 'thanks'. She walked quickly to the internet café where she knew she'd be able to call the number in Addis.

The phone began to ring. Once, twice, three times. Then on the fourth ring, a woman answered, "Hello?"

"Hello, this is Zoya from Adama. Is this Eshe?"

"No. This is Kamali. How can I help you?"

Puzzled, Zoya said, "Oh, I was trying to contact my friend's cousin Eshe in Addis."

"I know Eshe, but she's not here right now. She's in our training program. Is there something I can do to help you?"

Hesitating, Zoya continued, "I was told Eshe was going to be working for a modeling agency and your company needed another girl."

"Yes, that's correct. Do you know someone who may be interested?"

Her palms felt sweaty and her heart was beating faster, "Yes, I might be interested."

"Wonderful. I'll need three things from you. Send me a shoulder-up photo of yourself as well as a full body photo in a blouse and skirt. Also, I'll need a brief résumé along with contact information. Can you do that? Oh, how old are you?"

"I'm sixteen but will be seventeen in three months."
"Okay. I can't promise you anything but if you'll get me your information, we can see what happens. I'll give you an email address where you can send your photos and résumé."

Behati snapped the required photos and Zoya completed a quick résumé during her noon lunch, all of which she emailed to Addis. A quick response told her to check her email in three hours for an update.

The afternoon drug on. Finally, the last class was over. Zoya and Behati quickly went to the internet café to check for the email. Logging on, they waited. Then, there it was, waiting to be opened.

One click and the message appeared.

'Dear Zoya,

We received your photos and résumé. Thank you for being so prompt. We believe you're exactly the type of person we would like to add to our 'modeling group' and program. We have an immediate opening in our training program and would like to discuss details with you. Please call me at your earliest convenience at the same number you called before.

Sincerely, Kamali

Behati looked at Zoya and asked, "What are you going to do?"

With a smile, "I'm going to call them, of course!"

Again, the phone rang, but this time it was answered on the first ring.

"Hello, this is Kamali."

"Hello Kamali, this is Zoya from Adama."

"Oh yes. You must've received my email. Thanks for calling back. Do you still have an interest?"

"Possibly, but I do have a few questions."

"I'm glad you have questions. We like our models to be 'thinkers' not just 'beauty queens'. How can I help you?"

Zoya's most important question was blurted out, "What would I be paid for the work?"

Kamali replied with a number nearly double what she knew her father was earning at his hard labor.

"If I did accept your offer, could I contract for just one year?"

"Of course, but I'm certain, after one year, you'll know this will be your lifetime vocation."

Zoya asked, "How soon would you need me in Addis?"

"I have an immediate opening and would love to have you here as soon as possible. In fact, if you could get on the morning bus the day after tomorrow, that would be perfect. Can you do that?"

Zoya said, "Just a minute. I need to talk with my friend... "

Behati was listening to the conversation beside Zoya and whispered, "Wow! I'm beginning to wish I'd listened to Eshe and taken the opportunity. What do you think you should do?"

"I don't think there's a decision to make. That amount of money for my parents would make all the difference in the world! I'm telling her 'yes.'"

Back on the phone Zoya said, "I do have one more question. I could get there, but what about living expenses while I'm there?"

"Oh, I'm sorry, I forgot to tell you. All of your food and housing will be provided for three months on top of your salary. That will permit you to get on your feet. What do you think?"

"Okay. I'll be there the day after tomorrow."

"Great, welcome to a new world. I can guarantee you this job will open up a whole new life for you! I hope you enjoy traveling and learning new cultures because you'll be getting a lot of opportunities for that. I'll send you an email with our address and I'll see you soon!"

Zoya hung up the phone and looked at Behati. Then they both screamed and hugged each other.

Behati asked, "What are you going to tell your parents?"

"I'm not sure how it'll go but I'll tell them tonight at supper. It won't be easy, I'm sure."

Marjani said, "I made something special for dessert."

Zoya watched as her mom brought the Baklava to the table. She began spooning the warm dessert onto three dishes. The rich, thin pastry on top and bottom captured the fruits and nuts layered between them. The top was covered with warm honey.

Kojo said, "Angel, get me a napkin. My mouth is watering!"

Zoya laughed and accepted the delicacy placed in front of her.

Spooning the first bite into her mouth, she faced her first doubts about leaving her family. She'd miss the safety, security and love she was now feeling. Money could buy almost anything, but she knew love couldn't be purchased.

"Mom and Dad, there's something I need to talk to you about. Please listen until I'm done explaining."

She began by sharing the guilt and shame she'd been experiencing by watching her parents suffer over the years on behalf of her future and success. Then she told them what had happened in the last 24 hours and her desire to help support the family.

Finally finished, she waited.

Marjani stood and brought the Baklava back to the table. Spooning more onto Zoya's plate, she smiled and said, "You'd better have more of this because I doubt you'll find better in Addis."

Her mom continued, "I hope you understand this isn't something I want to see happen. I would've thought you'd come to us before making such a big decision. Your dad and I have been through a lot in life and we both have experiences to draw from and instincts about things. But it seems your mind is made up. Since you've told us you've already decided and told the woman you're coming, what are we to say?"

Kojo responded, "Angel, you know our entire lives are built around you. Without you around, we'll lose some purpose for working so hard. You mean everything to us. Like your mom said, I wish you'd have let us work through this with you." Pausing, he said, "I suppose we'll be able to visit you in Addis once in a while? Also, you said this is only a trial for a year? Will you promise to let us be a part of your decision a year from now?"

Zoya smiled and said, "Yes, I promise. This isn't the end of our family. I'm just taking advantage of an opportunity and I'll be sending you money once a month. I know I'll feel a lot better knowing I'm giving rather than just taking."

Looking at her father, Zoya smiled and said, "Dad, you know what I'm thinking right now, don't you?"

He smiled, nodded his head and said, "Yes, we've always known what the other was thinking. Right now you're thinking I married your mother when she was sixteen."

Zoya grinned and said, "See, we're still connected. That's exactly what I was thinking."

Kojo said, "Marjani's mom and dad weren't ready to let her go and said it was a bad idea for her to get married so young. Besides, what was I to do? She was so sweet I couldn't wait any longer. I think it's turned out okay?"

Marjani smiled and said, "It's been more than okay. All right, enough of this talk. Let's start getting your bags packed. Thirty-six hours from now you'll be on a bus!"

The good-byes to her mom and dad as well as to Dani, Behati and Anika had been tearful and difficult but finally behind her. The bus had just parked at the central bus station in Addis Ababa and she had her backpack in her hand. Looking around she saw a dozen blue and white cars parked in a line. Assuming they were taxis she approached the first one and gave the address to the driver. He smiled and said, "We'll be there in about twenty minutes."

As a first-timer in Addis, Zoya was amazed at the size of the city. In Adama, it took twenty minutes to drive from one side of the city to the other, but Addis seemed to go on and on.

The driver said, "We're at your address," as he slowed down and parked.

Zoya paid him and stood on the sidewalk in front of a large stone wall. The stones were multi-colored and precisely laid. She saw a blue, steel door inset in the wall and approached it.

Pausing as her new world was about to open, she knocked on the door. It was soon opened by a guard who smiled and said, "I'll bet you're Zoya! Kamali is expecting you. Come in."

Almost immediately a young woman came out of the home and joined them. "Zoya, it's so good to meet you! I hope your trip was okay. Welcome!"

Then apologetically she said, "Oh, I apologize. My name is Kamali. We've talked on the phone. Come in, come in! I want you to meet someone."

Passing through an immaculate and gorgeous courtyard surrounded by trees, shrubs and flowers they went up three steps to a wide veranda with a table, wicker chairs and other furniture.

Entering the home, Zoya couldn't believe how large the first room was. It was nearly as large as her home in Adama. She began to feel out of place. Immediately she remembered something her dad told her a few years ago. She'd come home from school one day after a student made fun of her clothing. Her personal self-worth had taken a beating that day and she felt resentful of her family's status or maybe lack of status. Her dad had said, "There's an old Ethiopian proverb that says, *'The elephant doesn't limp when walking on thorns.'*"

She'd asked him what it meant and he'd said, "You're my daughter! You're an angel and you're strong! Walk with your head held high even when you're in pain!"

"Zoya! You must be Zoya!"

Startled, Zoya turned and saw a middle-aged and elegant woman emerging from the kitchen. With a huge smile, the woman kissed her on both cheeks and said, "Welcome! My name is Subira. This is my home and it's yours for the next two weeks."

Then holding Zoya by her shoulders, she pushed her back at arm's length and said, "Kamali, you're so right. She's very photogenic and just what we're looking for. You have good instincts.

"Come, let me show you the house, your bedroom and introduce you to another girl."

Zoya said, "Thanks. Oh, speaking about the other girl, I heard that a girl named Eshe was here. I was hoping to meet her."

"Oh, I'm sorry, but Eshe began her new work this morning. She's on the other side of the city. She would have loved to meet you but her work began quickly."

Just then a young girl came down a magnificent staircase. Zoya was struck by the shy demeanor of the small girl. She stopped on the bottom step and Subira said, "Mariam, come here. I want you to meet Zoya. She'll be living here with us for another two weeks."

After meeting Mariam and taking a tour of the house, Zoya entered her bedroom and laid down on the soft bed. She couldn't believe her good fortune. She wished she could somehow share it with her mom and dad as she wondered what was next.

Chapter 3

Ropi, Central Ethiopia
3:30 p.m. – Tuesday, September 1, 2015

HANA

"IT'S bleeding! What should I do?"

Hana climbed over the rough lava terrain to her friend's side. Abena was sitting on the inner slope of an ancient volcano looking at her knee.

Hana said, "Oh, it's bleeding!"

Abena looked at Hana and quipped, "That's what I said. Didn't you believe me?"

"Well, what I meant to say is, 'it's bleeding a lot!'"

"That doesn't make me feel any better. What should we do?"

"We need to get you home. It's almost three miles and it's gonna take a while. But first we'll need to bandage it."

Hana looked down at her blue shirt and knew what she had to do. Peeling it off, she began tearing a two inch strip from the bottom. Putting the shirt back on, she turned her attention to the cut. A flap of skin was peeled back from the gash. Abena winced as Hana pushed it back into place. Noticing tear-filled eyes, Hana said, "Sorry. I'm not sure how to do this, but we need to stop the bleeding."

"I'll be okay. As my papa says, Ropi's are tough."

Life in central Ethiopia wasn't easy. The volcanic rock terrain wasn't overly conducive to growing crops though the farmers certainly tried. After all, the cattle they herded did need grain periodically as did the Ropi families.

Wrapping the strip of cloth around Abena's knee, she left enough material to tie a knot. Hana helped Abena to her feet and they began the 200 foot walk up the rough incline to the top edge of the volcano.

The inactive and ancient crater behind them was huge and almost a half-mile across. The water in it looked like black ink. Hana's dad said it wasn't because the water was dirty, it was because the crater was so deep.

Stumbling up the slope, Hana said, "We're almost to the top, then it's downhill and flat country the rest of the way. It won't be as tough. Maybe we can find a stick to help support you."

Finally at the top, they both dropped to the ground to rest. Looking far below at the water, Abena said, "We should have gotten some water to drink before we left. It's a long way home."

"I guess we weren't thinking about that, thanks to your bleeding knee."

"I'm sorry. I shouldn't have been running. I knew better, but going downhill I couldn't stop."

"I know. You're not the only one who's made that mistake."

"I'm really glad we're not able to go to school. We'd have less time to do this kind of stuff." Then Abena laughed and said, "Now we're able to herd cattle, plant maize and run up and down volcanoes."

Hana added, "...and tear up our knees. The kids who go to school will probably leave Ropi and not come back. For me, I love this area. But, I've never been anywhere else. Do you suppose this is like Heaven?"

Abena responded, "If this were Heaven we wouldn't be two crazy girls walking thru a desert, without water and with a bleeding knee. No, I don't think this is like Heaven."

They both laughed as they lurched toward home.

Ropi was just another small town in central Ethiopia. As with every other city or town, there were small villages of tukuls surrounding the town itself. These fringe villages housed the poorest of the people. The families in these outlying villages provided meat, grain and vegetables to the towns. It was just such a village Hana and Abena walked through as they finally arrived home.

The sun had set by the time Hana opened the wooden gate to Abena's home. Entering the round tukul, Abena dropped onto a rug on the ground next to the fire pit. Abena's mother quickly came to her daughter and said, "I wondered where you girls were and if something had happened." Then she exclaimed, "Baby, what happened to your knee?"

"Well, first of all, I'm not your baby. I might be your youngest but being thirteen years old isn't a baby."

"Yes Baby, I know. But what happened?"

"I fell at the crater and cut my knee. Hana bandaged it for me."

With a knife, Abena's mom cut the bandage loose and looked at the blood encrusted cut. "We'll need to wash it and see what else we need to do."

Grabbing a pan and filling it with water, she took a cloth and began dampening the clotted wound. Then gently she began washing it. It was evident the flap of skin would need to be stitched into place.

As her mom found the necessary items, Abena said, "My mom makes our clothes. I suppose she's as good as a doctor."

Hana looked at her friend and knew Abena was trying to mask her fear with some humor.

"I'm going to use my gold colored thread to sew this. Then I can call you my 'Golden Baby.'"

Tears trickled down Abena's face, but there were no gasps or murmurs as again and again the needle made its healing journey around the wound.

Finally finished, a thick layer of home-made ointment covered the gold-sutured flesh and a thick bandage was wrapped and tied over the wound.

"Golden Baby, you're going to have to be careful so the thread doesn't tear. We need to make sure the flesh knits together before the stitches are removed. I'm sorry to disappoint you, but your next visit to the crater will be weeks from now."

Abena wondered how long she'd need to put up with her new nickname.

Exhausted from the stress and the three mile hike, Hana walked the ten minutes to her own tukul. As she walked in, she inhaled the familiar smell of food, fire and cattle. That smell couldn't be reproduced anywhere else, she was sure. There was certainly a sense of security which came with these predictable and familiar odors. Her papa once told her, 'Women pay a lot of money for perfumes men can make, but there isn't any better smell than an Ethiopian tukul.'

"Hana. We've been worried. Where have you been?"

"Sorry Papa, but Abena fell at the crater and it took us longer to get home. Then, her mom had to sew the cut she had on her knee. Where's mama?"

"Oh, she was needed in the village to deliver a baby. She'll be back soon. We already ate our supper and yours is in the pot over the fire."

Ladling the heavy stew into a bowl, she bowed her head and thanked God for the food, friends and family.

Papa sat across the fire from her, watching her while she ate. He was forty years old and tired. Caring for his cattle while trying to eke out a living in the volcanic dry sand wasn't easy. It had taken its toll.

He looked at his youngest daughter and tenderly said, "Your mom and I are thankful for you. Your two sisters have their own lives to live now that they're married and moved away. You've done a lot for us by helping with the cattle and farming. I don't know what I'd do without you."

Hana looked up at her father. She'd not seen him like this before. She noticed a twinge of sadness in his eyes.

"What's the matter, Papa? Are you upset because I came home late?"

He looked at her and then diverted his eyes to the tukul's fire-pit between them.

"Hana, we learn a lot from our village elders. I heard them talk about an African proverb that says, *"More precious than our children are our children's children."*

With a confused look, she asked, "What does that mean?"

"As your papa I want to make sure you're taken care of so someday your children will have opportunities I never had. I've worked with cattle and grain all my life, just as my father and his father before him. You deserve better. I want you and your children to thrive. I think you'll need to leave Ropi for that to happen."

"But Papa, I love it here. This is my home and I love cattle and grain."

Hesitating, he continued, "I know that. But, life is difficult here and there could be so much more for you. Your mama and I have talked and we think it would be good for you to learn a trade and earn some birr on your own. We don't want to see you work hard all your life and have little to show for it. We want you and your children to have an easier life than we've had."

Hana's eyes narrowed and her voice whispered, "Are you thinking about sending me away?"

Hana had watched as several young people in her village left over the last few years and she was certain about one thing. They didn't return. There was no doubt among the villagers that when someone went to Addis Ababa, the capital, there were many jobs waiting for them. There seemed to be some sort of satisfaction among parents if they were able to get a child or two to Addis.

Papa said, "Hana, it's not 'sending you away', but rather 'giving you an opportunity'. Look around our tukul. What do you see? Mud walls. A dirt floor with a few rugs. Cattle and their fleas sleeping with us. A fire in the pit which is always lit and showering sparks into the air. You're inhaling smoke that isn't good for your lungs. You deserve better."

"But all the things you've talked about, except the fleas, are things I love about Ropi. You and Mama have a nice life and that's what I want too."

"Hana, our ancestors have always said, *'He who doesn't seize today's opportunity will be unable to seize tomorrow's opportunities'*. If we don't take the opportunity we're given today, there are no more opportunities for tomorrow. We have an opportunity today."

Again with a premonition, she whispered, "What do you mean? We have an opportunity today?"

He lowered his eyes to the fire and said, "A man came to our village today. He's looking for two or three young people to go with him to Addis Ababa to work in one of the textile mills. Your mom and I are thinking God has brought you this opportunity. We shouldn't pass it up."

Shocked, Hana simply looked at her father.

"You and Mama both think this is what's best? Sending me away?"

"Yes, we do. The world is changing around us and I think this village is stuck in time. It's an opportunity of a lifetime for you."

"When would I leave?"

"He's leaving mid-morning tomorrow."

Hana heard the familiar creaking of the opening gate in the yard and then the metal clink as the latch fell in place. Turning toward the door she saw the tired face of her mama entering the tukul.

Hana got up from her seat on the rug, hugged her mother and said, "Papa just told me I'd be leaving our village. Is that true? Are you sure this is what you want?"

Hugging her daughter, she said, "Hana, no, no, no. A thousand times no! This isn't what I want. I want you right here beside me for the rest of my life. But, we don't always get what we want. I agree with your papa. This is an opportunity for you we should take advantage of. But, we promise you, we'll stay connected and we'll come to see you in Addis in a few months. You'll see, this will be a good thing!"

Hana slowly went to her matte and laid down. She knew the decision was made. There would be no more discussion. Staring overhead, her eyes stung from the tears flowing down her cheeks. She savored the rich earthy aroma of cattle, dung and smoke. She heard the familiar grunting of the cattle as they stomped their hooves in the soft dirt just ten feet away. She swatted a fly buzzing near her ear and then fell asleep with apprehensions about the upcoming morning.

Hana opened the wooden gate which permitted the cattle to leave the tukul. Gently, she touched the face of each one as they filed past her. She gathered a few armfuls of loose hay and fluffed it into the feed trough. Carrying a small bucket of grain, she emptied it into the trough while being nudged by the cattle which were excited by the smell.

With a last look at the livestock, she retreated behind the tukul and washed with cold water and home-made soap. She paused as she soaked up the morning sun and crisp air.

Entering the tukul she retrieved her only dress and prepared for what was to come. Her mother watched her from the fire pit where she was preparing breakfast.

The door opened and Hana saw her papa enter with a man she'd never seen before. He wore a white shirt with a tie which was almost unheard of in her village. Hana assumed he was the man from the textile factory.

Mama welcomed him and asked him to sit down for breakfast, but the man nodded at Hana and said, "So, I'd suppose you're Hana?"

"Yes."

"Well, I'm pleased to meet you. My name is Omari. I'm from Addis Ababa."

Mama repeated, "Please, sit down. It's time for breakfast."

Hana's father said, "Omari, it's customary for us to ask God's blessing on our food and the day ahead of us. Would you do that for us?"

"Of course." He clasped his hands and shut his eyes and said, "Our Father God. We're deeply grateful for the hospitality of this family and ask You to bless them. We have food prepared and we ask You to bless it so we can do the things You ask of us. I thank You for Hana. I know this is a difficult time for her as she prepares to leave for Addis this morning. Place Your protective hands on her and keep her safe and happy. In Jesus' name we pray. Amen."

Mama began ladling a breakfast soup for the four of them and placed a plate of fresh bread on the rug-covered floor.

Omari said, "Hana, I want you to know something. Your mother and father are different than most parents I work with. Normally, we provide compensation to parents when we take their child to Addis for work. Your mom and dad refused to take the funds. Your papa told me, 'We only want Hana to have a great opportunity. If we took money, it'd seem like we're wanting her to leave because we want the birr. We only want her to have an opportunity to succeed'. As I said, your mama and papa are different. You're a very blessed girl."

Hana lowered her head. Right now she wasn't feeling blessed.

As they finished the morning meal, Omari stood and said, "Thank you for the wonderful breakfast. But all good things must come to an end. It's time for us to leave and we have 200 miles to travel today. I'll let you say your goodbyes and I'll see you outside."

Hana cried as she said good-bye to her mom and dad. Papa said, "Hana, you're thirteen and you've learned a lot. We think you're an adult who's capable of making good decisions. If you stay close to God, the Holy Spirit will be your guide and you'll be just fine. We'll see you in a few months."

Silently, Hana wondered about the double standard. Her dad said she was capable of making decisions, yet this wasn't something they had let her decide. For the first time in her life, Hana was getting acquainted with a new emotion. Resentment.

Mama gave her the hug of all hugs and then they walked outside into the warm sunshine. A car was parked fifty feet away. Omari was standing beside it. In the back seat were a boy and a girl about her age. Hana knew them from a neighboring village. She was thankful she wouldn't be alone for the trip to Addis.

Climbing into the back seat, she readied herself for her first car ride. As Omari steered the car down the village lane, Hana looked out the back window to get a glimpse of her mom and dad waving. Behind them was her home. Would she ever see it again?

They'd finally arrived in Addis Ababa and the mid-afternoon sun was still pushing its heat through the open windows. Hana couldn't believe the size of the city. Once they entered the capital city, they still drove an hour. Omari stopped in front of a compound surrounded by a stone wall. He opened the back door of the car and asked the boy to come with him. Hana watched as he fearfully got out. Carrying his small backpack, he followed Omari to a large gate.

Soon the gate opened and Omari and the boy disappeared inside. Five minutes later, Omari returned to the car alone.

Driving for another fifteen minutes, he stopped at yet another home. Again, Omari got out and asked the other girl to join him. The girl looked at Hana with fearful eyes and exited the car. Together, she and Omari vanished behind the wall.

Feeling very alone in the back seat, Hana was full of fear. It was the same fear she'd felt at night when she knew the hyenas were scouring the village looking for food scraps or unattended cattle. She thanked God many times for their tukul door, knowing how it protected her from whatever was on the other side. In the back seat of the car, she was feeling secure for the moment, but who knew what was next?

Omari returned and they drove to the front of another walled compound. He got out and opened Hana's car door. She followed him to a blue, steel door which was inset in an ornate wall of stone.

Omari knocked. After a long fearful minute, the door opened. The guard said, "Omari, it's good to see you." Then, looking at the thirteen-year-old, he asked, "Are you Hana?"

She was surprised a guard in Addis Ababa would know her name. Then she saw two women coming out of a magnificent home. They came to the gate. The older one said, "Hana, come in, come in! My name is Subira and this is my secretary Kamali. Welcome!"

They crossed a courtyard with an overhanging veranda and entered the front door of the home. Hana noticed two girls sitting on a sofa. They stood and Subira introduced them as Mariam and Zoya.

Omari left and Kamali said, "Girls, supper's ready. Please come to the kitchen."

Hana hesitantly said, "I'm sorry but I've been traveling and I need… "

Kamali said, "Oh, forgive me. Come with me Hana. I'll show you."

She opened a door to a brightly lit, white room. Hana entered it and the door closed behind her. She hadn't seen anything like it before, but raising the lid on the small white chair she understood what the water filled stool was for.

She looked for a bucket of water to wash her hands and found none. Seeing the white sink she pushed and pulled on the levers until water splashed into the basin. She washed her hands and dried them on a white towel. Then she began pushing and pulling the levers until the water stopped.

Joining the others in the kitchen, she sat down at the table. It was filled with meat, injera, vegetables and fruit. She bowed her head to thank God even though the others had already started eating.

The food was excellent and a cautious hopefulness began to creep into Hana's mind.

Subira said, "Hana, you'll be staying here for about two weeks. We'll be teaching you and the other girls some skills before you go on to your new work. I'm expecting three more girls this week, so in the meantime, just relax and enjoy yourself."

Finally, the cook passed a wonderful looking dessert and said it was called Baklava. Zoya said, "My mom made this for me the night before I left for Addis! It's my favorite dessert."

Hana looked at Mariam and wondered how someone, so young and vulnerable, could have been brought to this place. She seemed too small to work in a factory. There seemed to be a sadness buried in the black-eyed girl. Hana wondered what stories the other two girls could share about what had brought them to this place.

She pushed her plate forward for another serving of the Baklava dessert and smiled at Subira.

Chapter 4

Addis Ababa, Ethiopia
11:20 a.m. - Sunday, August 30, 2015

MAKDA

THE church was quiet as the four girls walked up the three steps to the stage. They nervously looked out at the three hundred people in the congregation.

It was a warm Sunday morning in Addis Ababa and the pastor's message had been about the 'Sermon on the Mount'. It was now firmly etched in the listener's minds. Makda and her three best friends had been invited to sing while the offering plate would make its collective rounds among the pews.

Their soft and beautiful voices blended well, which wasn't surprising as they'd been singing together since they were twelve years old.

Their arms linked, they sang as if they were 'one'. The music, words and harmony always touched the hearts of the church members. It was obvious the girls loved their Lord, music and each other. They named their group *'Holy Spirit Harmony'*.

The girls walked off the stage and sat in their pew. The pastor returned to the podium, waited for the perfect moment and quietly said, "If my eyes had been shut, I'd have thought God sent four angels to our church this morning!"

The last prayer was uttered and the church service was over. Makda said to her friends, "Come over to my place. I've got something to show you."

They stepped outside into the warm sunshine.

"Makda, Makda!"

The girls turned to see their pastor approaching with a box.

"Oh, I'm glad I caught you. Makda, you told me two weeks ago you needed more 'food', so I was able to get this for you. But you'll need to add your own 'salt.'"

The girls laughed as Makda asked, "Food? Salt? I don't remember asking you for anything."

With a smile, the pastor said, "Weren't you paying attention this morning in church as we read Matthew 5?"

Seeing Makda's rising confusion, he said, "I'm teasing you Makda. I know you were paying attention. In the 'Sermon on the Mount', Matthew 5 says, we as believers are the 'salt of the earth.'"

Opening the box, he showed her six stacks of small Bibles. "Here's your 'food'. It's guaranteed if you add the 'salt', God will bless whoever you give these to."

Makda, now understanding, smiled, took the box and said, "Thank you Pastor, I'll do my best."

He looked at the other girls and said, "Let me know if you'd like some Bibles to share with others. I'll have more in a couple of weeks."

He continued, "When I look at the New Testament, I'm always amazed how the followers of Christ took His Gospel message to the world. Those Jesus followers were scattered like 'seeds in the wind' and they took His Word wherever they went."

Looking at the four girls, he continued, "You never know where God will take you, but one thing's for sure, He'll go with you wherever you go. Hide His Words in your hearts and you'll always have them when you need them."

They began their ten minute walk to Makda's home. Opening the gate to the small dirt yard, she unlocked the front door and stepped inside.

The home had a small bedroom, kitchen, bathroom and living area. It was small but clean, neat and comfortable.

A year earlier, Makda's dad had been killed in a car accident and her mother severely injured. Three days later her mom passed away and Makda was suddenly alone. Now eighteen-years-old, she wondered if she was too old to be considered an orphan.

Feigning impatience, Fana said, "Well, are you going to fix us coffee or not?"

Startled, Makda looked at her and said, "No."

Surprised but smiling, Fana replied, "Well, that's not being a very good hostess!"

"I've got something better!"

Going to her small refrigerator, she retrieved four cans of soda and pulled out a tray of cookies from the cupboard. Placing them on the kitchen table, she said, "Hope this is good enough?"

"Oh yeah," Fana said, "This'll do just fine!"

Jamila said, "Makda, I forgot to give you a message from our high school math teacher, Mr. Abebe. He said he misses you in class."

Makda smiled.

Tezeta said, "He's not the only one who misses you at school. We're all sad you had to drop out after your parents died. But we understand and we're glad you were able to get a job and keep your home."

Makda looked at her three best friends and smiled. Then she said, "With my dad gone, there wasn't any money to pay for books and tuition. When I was able to get the cleaning job at the office building, I was able to at least pay my bills."

Pausing, she said, "There's something else I want to talk to you about.

"I'm really happy to have my job, but it's probably not going to be enough. Dad inherited this house from his dad and mom so it's been in the family a long time. But several days ago I received notice the city is going to tear down this neighborhood and build apartment buildings. They've been doing that all over the city and it looks like ours is next. They'll be paying me for my home, but it won't be enough to buy another home like it. Rent is really high since so many people are looking for a place to stay. I'm going to have to do something different."

Fana asked, "So, what are you going to do?"

"That's the reason I wanted to talk to you."

Getting up and walking to the counter, she picked up a glossy brochure. Holding it up, they read the bold print – *'Travel Abroad – Employment Available in Riyadh'*.

"Riyadh? Where's that?"

Jamila answered Fana, "Don't you remember your geography lessons in fourth grade? Riyadh is the capital city of Saudi Arabia."

Fana said, "Wow! Saudi Arabia, that's a long way from here."

Makda replied, "It's just across the Red Sea."

"Yeah right! Don't you remember your Bible stories? The children of Israel were trying to escape Egypt and the Pharaoh. They almost drowned trying to get across the Red Sea."

"But they didn't drown. They escaped."

As they realized Makda was serious, Tezeta quietly said, "Makda, I don't think this is a good idea. That's a long way from Addis."

Makda replied, "I'm not sure you understand how lonely I feel without my mom and dad. You know what happens here in Addis if you're a young woman and can't earn enough? I'm going to lose my home and I don't even have a high school diploma. I need to think ahead. I've been asking God for direction on what path to take and then I found this brochure at the bus stop. It was like an answer to prayer."

Tezeta was reading the brochure and asked, "Are you going to call them to see if you qualify?"

Looking at her friends, Makda replied, "I called them yesterday and I have an appointment tomorrow."

The girls continued talking for another hour and then left. Makda once again felt very alone and vulnerable.

~~~~~~~~~~

Entering the office lobby, Makda told the secretary, "My name is Makda and I have an appointment at ten o'clock."

Scrolling down a printed list, the secretary stopped at her name and said, "Ah, yes, here it is. Take a seat and fill out this questionnaire."

Taking the three-page document to a chair, Makda sat down. Looking around the room, she saw two other girls busy filling out their own paperwork.

Soon a door opened and a girl emerged followed by a middle-aged woman. The woman called a name and one of the two waiting girls followed her into an office.

Twenty minutes later the scene repeated itself.

Finally, the woman entered again and said, "Makda?"

She stood and followed the woman into a plush office. The woman said, "My name is Hilina. Welcome." Pointing to a chair, she said, "Please sit down."

She began to feel like a bug under a microscope.

Hilina studied the paperwork on her desk and finally said, "Let's talk about why you're here."

Makda shared her circumstances. Hilina listened intently and then asked, "So, you don't have any family here in Addis?"

"I have an Uncle Gyasi, but I don't know him very well. He's an attorney but has a large family to take care of. So, even though he's family, he's unable to help me. I'm on my own."

"I'll need you to put his contact information on this form in case of an emergency. Do you have a passport?"

"No, I don't even have a driver's license."

"Makda, just looking at your paperwork and hearing your situation, I'm sure I can get you employment in Saudi Arabia. It's a long way from here and a very different culture. Are you sure this is what you want to do?"

"I don't think I have a choice. With the amount of money I can make there in one or two years, I can return here with experience and money saved. If you think this work is a fit for me, I'm ready to go."

Hilina replied, "Okay. It'll take me two weeks or so to get all your paperwork ready, including your passport and visa. In the meantime I have a place for you to stay in preparation for your trip to Riyadh. There's a woman I use to prep girls for living abroad. I'd like for you to get your things in order, come back Friday at noon and I'll get you into training. Okay?"

Relieved, yet apprehensive, Makda replied, "Yes, I'm excited. Thanks so much for the opportunity. I'll be here."

Walking home, Makda made a mental checklist of all she'd need to do over the next few days. First, she needed to have her uncle take care of the house situation. As an attorney, he'd be able to deal with the local government concerning the home payment and getting the furniture removed and sold. There really wasn't much else to do other than packing a few things and saying good-bye to her friends.

Makda arrived at the employment office ten minutes early. She carried a backpack loaded with some clothing, a few personal things and the twenty-four small Bibles. She was instructed to wait in the lobby.

Finally, twenty minutes later, Hilina arrived and said, "Looks like you're ready to go. Let's get your things down to the car and I'll take you to where you'll stay for the next two weeks."

As they got in the car, Hilina said, "When you get to Riyadh, the family you'll work for will be getting you everything you need. You'll be well taken care of."

Makda smiled. She was going to miss her friends and her church family but she was thankful for the hope of a bright future.

Thirty minutes later Hilina pulled the car to the curb in front of a large compound with a blue gate. Grabbing her pack, Makda stood at the gate with Hilina. Her knock was answered quickly by a guard who greeted them with a smile. "Hilina and Makda. Welcome. I'll get Subira."

Soon, the guard returned with two women who introduced themselves as Subira and Kamali. It was evident the two women knew Hilina very well as Kamali asked, "How's your son doing? Was the doctor able to diagnose his fevers?"

She answered, "That's kind of you to remember. They found out it was Yellow Fever. He's doing better but it'll take a while for him to get his strength back. I'm not used to seeing him in bed all day."

Hilina continued, "Subira, we'll have someone pick Makda up in two weeks for her trip to Riyadh. In the meantime, thanks for doing your usual great job of prepping her for the job."

"No problem. That's what I do. This round I'll have six girls training at the same time. Thanks again."

As Hilina left, three girls with smiles came from the house and stood on the veranda. Kamali introduced them as Mariam, Zoya and Hana as they gave their customary kisses to Makda's cheeks.

Chapter 5

West Central Highlands, Ethiopia
7:30 a.m. – Thursday, September 3, 2015

LOLA and MAYA

THE forest was quiet and damp from the overnight dew. It was the best time of the day for Lola and Maya as they climbed the green-forested mountainside walking toward their family's coffee plants.

Their almost daily ritual of tending coffee plants kept them and their families very busy. As cousins they were inseparable. Though younger than Maya by one year, Lola was the leader of the two, as Maya had always been more reserved and cautious. Their personality traits were evident to everyone who knew them.

Maya at thirteen and Lola at twelve had both gone through five years of public school but now their families needed them in the highlands. Two hundred miles west of Addis Ababa, the 6,000 feet elevation was ideal for growing coffee in the Goji region of west central Ethiopia.

Their family had inherited ten acres of land and coffee plants from their parents as did their parents before them. The region around them was filled with small independent farmers as well as large coffee plantations.

Though there were countless villages in the highlands, the forests had continued to survive. The valleys and slopes were spotted with the coffee groves. Without the coffee, poverty would have swallowed up the mountain dwellers decades ago.

While many families derived their income from growing and harvesting their beans, others were employed at the large coffee bean wash stations in the region. The pulping machines which removed the skin of the raw coffee bean, as well as the washing machines and tanks accommodating the twenty-four hour fermentation process, required many employees.

The weather in their Goji region permitted two crops per year to be grown. In many other areas only one crop per year would be produced so Lola's and Maya's families felt fortunate.

As the beans ripened, Lola and Maya would selectively pick the ones which were ready and leave the rest for additional ripening. The next day they'd return to pick more.

Planting, weeding, picking and sorting kept the girls busy. But, their love for one another made the days seem short. Their routine was predictable and they were happy, as long as they could be together.

Then things changed.

Chattering as always, they approached their small village, carrying the heavy burlap sacks on their backs which held the day's harvest.

Maya asked, "I wonder who the visitor is?"

Lola looked through the trees and noticed a car near Maya's small home.

Going to a small building behind her home, Maya opened the door and set her bag on the concrete pad, as did Lola. They'd empty the sacks and spread the beans out for sorting later, but now they raced each other to the house to see who was visiting.

Bursting through the front door, Maya with a yell said, "Aunt Aisha!"

She hugged Aisha quickly just as Lola shouted again, "Aunt Aisha!"

Aisha was just as excited to see her two nieces as they were to see her. She was the older sister of Maya's mother and Lola's father. She loved seeing them grow up, though those occasions didn't happen nearly often enough. Unable to have children, she doted on her nieces any chance she had.

"How long are you staying?" asked Lola.

"Lola, I'm surprised at you! I just arrived and now it sounds like you're ready for me to leave."

"No, that's not what I meant. You know how much we love having you visit. So, how long are you staying?"

"Well, I'd like to stay forever. I really miss these mountains. Addis Ababa isn't a bad place to live but for a rough and tough old mountain girl like me, it's too crowded. It can get really hot there and there's nothing like the clear, crisp air of the highlands to get my blood flowing! But, you know how your Uncle Amadi is. He needs me. I think I spoil him a little bit too much. So, I need to go back tomorrow."

Lola laughed and said, "We know you too. You miss him, I'll bet!"

Maya's mom abruptly said, "Go on girls. Get those beans sorted."

The girls left and Aisha said, "Now, where were we? Oh, that's right, you were going to get Negasi."

"I'll ask Lola to get her dad."

Maya's mother went to the door and hollered, "Lola!"

"Yes, Aunt Faizah", came the reply from the bean house.

"Run and get your papa. Aisha wants to talk to him."

Lola headed into the village. Three minutes later Lola and Negasi were back.

Lola ran down the path to Maya while Negasi gave the customary cheek pecks to his sister Aisha and asked, "How's Amadi?"

"He's been busy and doing well. He told me to say hello."

Looking around to make sure Lola and Maya had left, she continued. "I know you're all very busy with your beans, but I wanted to share something with both of your families. I wonder if you've ever thought about sending Maya and Lola to Addis. The textile mills are hiring like never before. They have international contracts to fill and they can't get enough employees for all the work. The pay is really good and the work is steady.

"I've often wondered how you're able to make it here financially. I know the coffee bean market is growing, but so is competition. I just heard about two more plantations coming on stream in the Goji region. The large plantations own the wash plants so you're at their mercy when it's time to sell your beans. It's probably just a matter of time before the small farmers will have no market for their beans. If the girls worked at the textile mills, they'd learn a trade and they would be able to send money back to you. Amadi and I would look in on them for you and make sure they're okay."

Negasi thought a bit and then said, "I don't know... but it's not the first time we've thought about something like that for Lola. As she gets older I wonder about her future. Coffee beans are all we know and it's hard work. I don't like the idea of Lola not getting a vocation. She deserves more than what these mountains can give her.

"One of my biggest concerns has been that no one would look after her in Addis. Anyone her age needs someone to keep track of them. And you know Lola, she doesn't know a stranger and trusts everyone. She's always ready for a fun time which isn't good. If Maya went with her and if you and Amadi took responsibility for them, we'd consider it."

Faizah said, "We've talked about it too. It seems the world is changing a lot. The best education and employment seems to be in the cities. It's hard to say what's going to happen to the small independent coffee growers like us. Like you said, more and more plantations are coming in and cutting us out. We can't contract with world buyers like they can. You're right Aisha, we're at the mercy of the plantations and we don't like that."

"One thing I know for sure, Amadi and I would love to spend more time with the girls. Why don't you talk to your spouses and the girls and let's see what they think."

Negasi said, "So, how does this work? If you took them to Addis, what happens next? Where do they stay?"

"Amadi knows a man who recruits young people to work in the mills. We'd take the girls to him and he'd find them work. He told us there's many other opportunities for good, strong and healthy young men and women. So, whether it's in the mills or working as a domestic for a wealthy family, there's no end to the jobs.

"If they work in the textile mills, there are dorms for the workers to live in. They get free room and board as part of their employment so they have almost no expenses.

"If they work as a domestic, they live with the family and of course, room and board would come with the job."

Maya's mom Faizah replied, "Seems pretty safe and simple. Maybe I need to come along and get a job!"

Negasi laughed and said, "If the girls go to the capital, we're going to need you picking beans!"

Aisha said, "Talk through it and let me know what you're thinking." Then, looking at Faizah, she continued, "It's been a long time since I've made a highlands meal so let me get supper started for you!"

The next morning, Maya and her parents along with Lola and her parents sat down together for an Aisha-prepared breakfast. After they were finished, Aisha asked, "Well, what are you thinking about my proposal?"

Faizah began. "Firew and I talked late last night with Maya. Going to Addis seems like the thing to do, but we all know Maya's personality. She's careful and cautious and very different than Lola. I suppose their differences are what makes them such good friends."

She looked at Maya and continued, "She's not the type to make changes quickly, so this would be a huge step for her. The decision is hers to make. At thirteen, she's mature and we trust her judgment."

Aisha said to Maya, "What are you thinking?"

Hesitantly she replied, "Mom was right in all she said, but I want to hear what Lola, Aunt Liya and Uncle Negasi have to say before I decide."

Negasi looked at Lola and said, "We talked last night and Lola's pretty excited about moving to Addis. We have our concerns, but the plan you shared takes away most of our fears. Lola, tell them what you're thinking."

Lola, with obvious excitement on her face said, "Yes, I'd like to go. I suppose if it doesn't work out and we want to return to our families, we could do that?"

"Of course. This is just a trial."

"Then I'm ready to go."

Everyone turned to Maya.

There was no excitement or smile on her face as she said, "I'll go with Lola. We've always done things together, so we may as well do this together too."

Aisha smiled. "Girls, I'm excited for your futures! I think Allah will bless your decisions."

Then she quickly added, "We need to leave soon so we can get to Addis by dark."

It didn't take long for the girls to pack and say their good-byes to their parents. The trip to Addis took about seven hours. Spending the night at Aisha and Uncle Amadi's home was something they wouldn't forget. Neither Lola nor Maya could comprehend how beautiful and large their home was. Coming from their highlands home with concrete floors to a home like Aisha's was more than they could have imagined.

Maya asked Lola, "Do you think someday we might live in a place like this? Just look at all that carpet and tile!"

"If Aunt Aisha could leave our village and live like this, I don't know why it couldn't happen to us. Getting a job and making money will be the first step!"

In the morning, after breakfast, Aisha said, "A man we know will be here soon to take you to a place that trains girls. You'll spend a couple of weeks learning before you start your new jobs. We'll get to see you in another month or so."

There was a knock at the front gate. Amadi hurried from the table and soon ushered in a middle-aged man. "This is Ajani. He's an agent who finds employees for a lot of factories and domestic workers for families."

Ajani received the customary kisses on his cheek from Maya and Lola and said, "I'm sure you're going to love being in Addis. The jobs I've got in mind for you are going to be just perfect."

Ajani stopped at a small restaurant after a thirty minute drive through the streets of Addis. He said, "Girls, stay in the car, I'll be back in a few minutes."

Maya said, "I could never have imagined how large Addis was! It seems like there's no end to cars, houses and streets."

Lola replied, "Remind me never to get lost here! It seems like we're a million miles away from our coffee plants!"

Ajani returned and said, "Come on inside with me and I'll get you something to drink. Someone will be coming soon to pick you up and take you to the training site."

Entering the small restaurant, Ajani ordered a cold cola for each of them. Pointing to a small table he said, "You can sit there and wait."

Ever the cautious one, Maya asked, "But how will we know this person who will pick us up?"

"Oh, they'll know your names. Everything's fine. I just don't have the time to take you all the way across the city."

The colas arrived and Ajani left the restaurant. Soon, they saw his car leaving.

"Didn't that seem a little strange to you?"

Lola replied, "I suppose, but like he said, he ran out of time."

Maya said, "How will Aisha and Amadi know where we're at? They know Ajani but he's not taking us to the next place. Do you think Aunt Aisha even knows where we're going?"

Lola replied, "Maya, I think you worry too much. Aisha's got this figured out."

As they drank their soft drinks, they continued to watch people coming and going. Then, a young woman approached their table and asked, "Maya and Lola?"

Lola responded, "Yes, that's us."

"My name is Taci. Ajani called me and asked me to take you to the training center. Are you finished with your drinks?"

Lola stood up and quickly said, "Yes. We're ready to go."

Grabbing their small bags, they followed Taci to a car parked nearby.

As they drove away, Taci said, "Why don't you girls tell me about your families and where you came from."

The girls began their stories and after many questions and fifty more minutes, Taci parked her vehicle outside a compound. Maya and Lola noticed a large stone wall with a blue steel gate.

They emerged from the car with their packs while Taci knocked on the gate. Quickly the door opened and the guard said, "Taci, you were just here last month and you're back again!"

"Yeah. Subira needed two more girls."

Subira came down the steps of the porch and said, "Taci, it's good to see you again. I presume these girls are Maya and Lola?"

"Yes, safe and sound. They've been traveling for a couple of days, so I'm guessing they're tired and ready to settle in."

With a huge smile, Subira said, "Maya and Lola, it's good to have you here. You'll enjoy the next two weeks with us. Come along and I'll introduce you to the other girls."

The girls looked at one another as they tried to fathom the beauty of the compound. They dutifully followed Subira and entered the spacious and gorgeous home. Sitting in the first room were four girls.

Subira said, "Girls, why don't you introduce yourselves to Maya and Lola?"

With a broad smile, the first girl said, "Hi, my name is Zoya. I'm sixteen and I came from a city south of Addis called Adama."

The second girl was small with beautiful black eyes. Timidly she said, "I'm Mariam. I'm nine years old and my village didn't have a name, so I don't know where I came from."

The third was an older girl who seemed very confident. She was smiling and seemed to be at home. "My name is Makda and I'm eighteen. I've always lived in Addis."

The last girl was young, shy and obviously unhappy. She wasn't angry or defiant, just sad. "I'm Hana and I came from a small village in south Ethiopia called Ropi. I'm thirteen."

Subira, with a smile, said, "Every two weeks we begin training for another group of trainees. Sometimes boys, sometimes girls. But it's usually six in the group. So, girls, we'll eat lunch and then we'll begin some training. It's time to get to work!"

PART 2

Life at Subira's Home

Weeks 2 - 3

September 7 – 21, 2015

Chapter 6

Addis Ababa, Ethiopia – Subira's Home
12:15 p.m. – Monday, September 7, 2015

SUBIRA watched with satisfaction as the girls chattered among themselves as they ate their lunch.

She'd learned over the years to watch quietly and assess the girls when they were least aware. Meal times were the ideal times to watch and learn. In a group, the girls let their guards down and became more transparent.

She'd become adept in determining personality traits, emotional strengths and weaknesses as well as any potential trouble-makers in the many groups she'd trained over the years.

She'd observed Mariam, the nine year old country girl, as being always quiet and not making eye contact. She was obviously the most vulnerable in the group and she'd need to have one of the other girls become Mariam's big sister for the next two weeks. The 'big sister' would have to be one who was obviously happy for the opportunities ahead. She thought Makda or Zoya could do the job. Maybe both of them, since they were equally excited to move forward with their futures.

As she watched Maya, she knew she had a melancholy personality and would be the most cautious and suspicious of the group. Subira had watched her quietly listening and watching the other girls in their continual conversations. Knowing Maya was the type who needed to process what was being said before acting, meant she was likely a skeptic. Subira realized some of the other girls would need to help Maya accept what was ahead.

Then there was Lola. It seemed obvious Maya needed her younger cousin more than Lola needed Maya. Subira knew she'd need to challenge Lola's independent streak and personality as soon as possible. She was a free-spirit and with what was ahead, she'd need to challenge that independence. If she didn't accomplish the task, Lola's future boss would do it in a way that would be much more hurtful. Dealing with free-spirited girls was never easy. When the group was together she'd create an opportunity to nudge Lola toward a more balanced personality.

Hana, a thirteen-year-old country girl, was going to need special care. Obviously she wasn't happy to be at Subira's. That wasn't unexpected, as 75% of the girls coming through her home had been brought against their will. A few of the girls, such as Makda and Zoya, came of their own free will to take advantage of an opportunity for their future.

The conversation started to die down as the girls finished their desserts. Then it grew quiet. It was as if the girls were silently asking, 'What's next'?

Subira filled the silence and said, "Girls, the maid will clean the kitchen. Let's go to the family room and talk."

As the girls settled into the sofas and large chairs, Subira began. "Two weeks from today, you'll each leave here to begin your new jobs. As the next two weeks go by, I'll observe you and eventually decide which jobs will be yours. I have many employers contacting me for workers and I'm known as someone who can meet their needs. We don't randomly place someone in just any job. We look at your particular personalities and talents and then place each of you accordingly.

"Many agents like me can provide workers, but you're different because you're getting two weeks of training that will make you very special. Young men and women are coming to Addis every day from all over the country searching for employment without this training. I'm giving you something different. You'll be trained in ways that make you stand out among the other job applicants. You're not ordinary girls. You're special. When someone leaves my training, they go to the top of our employer's lists.

"So, this afternoon, I'm going to give each of you an opportunity to share about your family and where you've come from. Then, I'll let each of the other girls ask you questions. After today, we won't be talking about your family or your pasts. The rest of your time with me will be about your future."

She looked at the group, knowing exactly what would happen next. "Which one of you would like to start?"

Mariam, Maya and Hana looked down. Zoya and Makda looked at each other. Lola immediately said, "I'll start."

Subira looked at her and said, "Okay Lola. I'll start by asking you a question. Why do you think it's okay for you to go ahead of Zoya or Makda who are quite a bit older than you?"

Lola didn't even blink, "You asked which one of us would like to start and the rest were hesitating. My father taught me a proverb that said, *'He who waits for another man's bowl, will eat late'*. She laughed out loud and looked at the other girls.

Subira smiled and said, "Oh. My father used proverbs too. He said, *'The person who hurries eats goat. The one who waits eats beef.'*"

Bristling, Lola said, "But, I like goat better than beef anyway. I don't mind going first."

Subira intentionally looked at Makda and said, "Makda, why don't you tell us about your family and why you're here?"

Deflated, Lola looked down at the rug for a moment then looked at Subira who was purposefully looking at Makda.

Makda began and the girls listened to her story of losing her parents in a car accident and how she then lost her home. They sat mesmerized as they heard about her desire to go to Riyadh, Saudi Arabia to work as a domestic worker and nanny for a family.

When she was finished the girls had a few questions for her, but soon Subira said, "Thanks Makda. Your losses and life experiences will make you a very successful person in Riyadh."

Then turning to Zoya, she said, "Explain how your situation in life brought you to Addis."

The girls listened intently as they heard Zoya's story of leaving her home because she wanted to financially help her parents. Fascinated, they heard about Zoya phoning Subira's secretary Kamali about a 'modeling' career. Becoming a photographer's model seemed pretty exotic to the younger girls who had several questions.

Then Subira said, "Hana, tell us about yourself."

Lola looked at the rug as she was obviously being pushed to the end of the speaking list.

Hana looked at her feet and whispered, "I'm not sure what to say."

Subira said, "Hana, I'm sure you have a lot to share. Tell us about your mother first of all. You'll have to look at us and speak louder so we can hear your story."

Hana reluctantly looked up for just a moment. Again, she looked down. When she finally looked up, she looked at Zoya and began talking. Subira knew who Hana's 'big sister' was going to be.

She talked about their family's tukul, the farming, cattle and the hard life on the volcanic plains. As she talked, she gradually loosened up and it was as if there was a two way conversation going on between Hana and Zoya.

Zoya had the first question for Hana, "Are you missing your family?"

Hana began crying and Zoya got up and sat beside her. Putting her arm around her, Hana quietly cried.

Subira said, "Thanks Hana for sharing. We know you miss your family. You had a lot to say and we feel sorry for what you've been through. I'm sure Zoya will help you with how you're feeling."

Then, "Maya, it's your turn. Tell us about your life."

Maya hesitated and looked at Lola. Subira said, "Don't worry Maya, Lola will get her turn. You're older and I want you to tell your story first."

Maya began by sharing how much she loved her time in the coffee grove highlands with Lola. "I've never known life without her or the coffee bean work. I was really disappointed when my mom and dad thought I should come to Addis. I was content in my village, but I also knew Lola would love a change and enjoy the opportunity to come here."

She smiled as she looked at Lola and continued, "Lola has always been the one who loved excitement and it was always me holding her back. I knew I couldn't forgive myself if I held her back from this opportunity. So, here I am."

"Thanks Maya. I wish I had friends like you. You're a very devoted person. I'm sure Lola appreciates you very much.

"Let's see, Mariam, why don't you go next?"

Lola was noticeably hurt as Subira was making her go last. Even more hurtful was that Mariam was only nine years old and three years younger than herself. This wasn't making any sense!

Mariam was incredibly shy. Before she uttered her first word, her eyes were glistening with tears which rolled down her cheeks.

Makda moved across the room and sat on the sofa beside Mariam.

Subira felt self-satisfied as she watched her prediction of Makda becoming Mariam's big sister fulfilling itself right before her eyes.

Makda took over by whispering to Mariam, "I'm here with you. You don't need to worry. Everything's good. Why don't you tell us about your papa?"

Mariam slowly began talking while Makda encouraged her to speak louder. She gently nudged Mariam's chin until she was looking into Makda's eyes.

Her words came more quickly as she began talking about her mom and dad. When she began sharing about her six-month-old baby sister Neela, the tears began and Makda held her close.

As she described what happened at the bus station with her escape from Baldy, the girls listened attentively. Makda's eyes filled with tears as the vulnerable nine-year-old blurted out the terror she'd encountered and the filth and stink of the meat vendors booth.

When Mariam was done, the room was quiet. Subira knew exactly what would happen next. She'd been through all of this before. Not once. Not twice, but many times. She knew the next question and she knew who would ask it.

"Subira, I don't have any questions for Mariam, but... "

"Yes, Makda. What is it?"

Makda continued, "I do have a question for you."

"Of course. Go ahead."

"Zoya and I are here because we chose to be here. But, Hana, Maya, Lola and Mariam didn't have that choice. I think I understand why Hana, Lola and Maya's parents chose to send them here, but Mariam was kidnapped and brought here in a horrifying way. Why are you involved with what's happening with her?"

The girls turned their heads to look at Subira. She smiled as she thought about the predictability of these girls. The question hung heavily in the air as Subira viewed the skeptical judge and jury who were all looking at her!

"Thanks for asking Makda. That's a very good question. I'm known in Addis Ababa for the work I do. My reputation is good and I don't want that to change. Let me share some things with all of you so you know what's happening."

She began by saying, "Mariam, do you remember what I told you about my past on the first day you were here?"

Mariam nodded her head.

"Well, now it's time to tell my story to the rest of you. First of all, I grew up in the country. It was north of here and life was very difficult. My family rarely had enough to eat and I was unable to go to school.

"I was given the opportunity to come to Addis to work and it was the best thing that ever happened to me. The hardest part was leaving my family, but I was soon able to send them money and help them out. I've decided to live my life in a way where I can help young girls like you have a better life."

Makda asked, "But were you kidnapped like Mariam?"

"No, I wasn't kidnapped. My situation was like Hana. My parents were very willing to have me go to Addis but I didn't want to come."

Makda pressed on, "So, it's not the same as Mariam's story. Can you explain why Mariam is here and why it looks like you're supporting kidnapping?"

Subira replied, "I think I can explain it. As I said before, I'm well known for my work here in Addis. Because of that, it's not uncommon for traffickers to bring me children or young men and women for employment opportunities.

"I always take them in. Believe me, they're better off with me than staying with the criminals who brought them here. I always try to find out as much as I can about where the child came from if they were brought here against their will. Unfortunately, there's a lot of this stuff happening and it's a profitable business for those who are doing it.

"I have many friends in the government and police force. I share my information with them. Sometimes we find a way to get the children back to their home. Sometimes we get the traffickers arrested. Unfortunately many of the children don't know where they came from."

Looking at Mariam, she asked, "Honey, do you know where you came from?"

"No, just that it took me two days to get here. I know there was a large city along the way where we got on a bus but I don't know the city's name."

Subira asked again, "Do you know if it was north, south, east or west of Addis?"

"No, I don't know. If I'd been able to go to school I probably would have learned my directions. At home I only needed to know two things. Where's my home and where's the river?"

"Makda, do you see how complicated it becomes? I do my best to make sure each of you are treated well and can get back home if you want to."

Looking at Mariam, she continued, "We're going to do our best to get you back home as soon as we can. I've already talked to the police about the man you call Baldy. We're going to get this taken care of. No one, especially a young girl like you, should ever have to go through what you've been through."

Then looking around the room, she said, "Well girls, that took about all afternoon and dinner will be ready at 6:00. You can rest until then."

"Subira?"

"Yes Maya?" She smiled as she already knew the question and who it would come from.

"We haven't heard Lola's story yet."

"Oh my, yes! Please Lola, share your story with us all, but keep it brief as supper will be ready soon."

Lola, looking like a deflated balloon, shared her story. It was brief and all the girls felt sorry for her as she finished.

Subira felt satisfied. Lola was one who enjoyed being in the spotlight and didn't enjoy being in the shadows. Deflating her ego had been necessary so she would learn submission. With a self-satisfied smile, Subira knew things were under control. She watched the girls as they disappeared up the stairs.

"Are you doing okay?"

Mariam looked up at Makda. After what she'd been through the last few days, it wasn't going to be easy to trust anyone.

Then, again Makda gently asked, "Mariam, are you okay?"

Hesitantly she said, "I think so. Thanks for sitting beside me this afternoon when Subira wanted me to talk. It was hard for me to say anything in front of the group, but you helped me."

"Do you want to talk some more before we go back down for dinner?"

Searching Makda's face, Mariam wondered if she could trust her.

Makda knew what she was thinking and said, "I've got an idea. Let's go outside to the courtyard. This house is getting stuffy."

They began descending the staircase to the first floor. Mariam touched the handrail and then grasped it with her hand. It felt just as smooth as some of the limbs on the acacia trees at the riverbank near her home. Quickly memories of her family flooded back. She could almost hear Neela's giggles. She could practically smell the sweet aroma of baking bread from their mud stucco hut. She remembered the sound of the flowing river with the wind blowing in the acacias.

There were noises in the kitchen as the cook was preparing their evening meal. Mariam followed Makda outside. Instead of sitting, Makda continued walking. Together they explored the garden and flowers. There was a small bench at the rear of the courtyard where they sat. Makda leaned back until she leaned against the stone wall. She closed her eyes as the late afternoon sunshine warmed her face.

Mariam asked, "What are you thinking about?"

Makda opened her eyes which now glistened with tears. "I'm missing my mom and dad. It's already been a year since they died and yet it still seems fresh. I'll never forget the day a police officer came to my school and told me my dad had been killed in a car accident and my mom was seriously hurt. He was so cold and matter-of-fact I nearly passed out.

"I remember the morning of the accident. I left the house in a hurry and barely had time to tell them good-bye. One of my regrets is I didn't take the time to give them each a hug and tell them I loved them."

Mariam leaned over and hugged Makda. They held one another for a full minute as they both cried.

Makda said, "I think we both needed that!"

Mariam smiled and nodded her head. Then she said, "Something happened this afternoon I wanted to talk to you about."

Makda looked down at Mariam and asked, "What is it?"

"You asked Subira a question about me being kidnapped, remember?"

"Of course. I was really bothered by how you were taken from your family and brought here. I knew I needed to ask her a few questions about the kidnapping, but I was taking a chance. If Subira was working with the traffickers I think she'd have been angry I was asking. But she wasn't angry.

"If Subira hadn't taken you in, I'm not sure where you'd be right now. It seems like Subira really wants to help. She said she'd shared with the police about the man who brought you here and that helped me better understand her heart."

Mariam said, "But one thing she said bothered me. Maybe there's a good answer, but it made me wonder about it. Subira said sometimes a trafficker brings her a kidnapped person and then she contacts the authorities."

"Yes, that's what she said."

"But, she already knew Baldy! When the gate opened the guard knew him and when Subira came out of the house she called him by his name, 'Tebeb'. She's known him all along and he's still kidnapping kids."

Makda's smile was gone. "I agree, that doesn't make sense. I'm going to ask her about it. If there's something wrong with this place, we'd better find out about it now rather than when it's too late. In the meantime, we'll listen and watch to see if anything isn't quite right. Okay?"

Mariam nodded her head and was relieved to know Makda was someone she could trust.

They could hear Subira calling the girls for dinner, so they quickly followed the path around the side of the home to the front door. Subira smiled as she saw Makda and Mariam coming into the house.

The other four girls came down the staircase laughing at something Lola had said. Upon seeing Subira, Lola stopped giggling.

During their dinner, Subira said, "We're going to have about ten days together, learning about your futures. But, I think it's important I share a quick lesson with all of you.

"This afternoon, I'm sure you noticed how I didn't let Lola begin our group conversation and I kept her until last. In fact, I acted like I'd forgotten her and then to top it off, I told her to be brief. All of that was very purposeful for her. It's my job to find the strengths and weaknesses in each of you. For you to survive on your own, you need to know your personal assets and flaws. We all have some of both, but it's not often anyone challenges our weaknesses. I'll be doing that with each of you and today it was Lola's turn. Each of you learned at Lola's expense.

"Lola's a leader and people are drawn to her. People listen to her and will follow her. That's a strength. But, it's a weakness when strong people push themselves ahead of others. Lola, it's not a weakness to follow and it's not a weakness to encourage others to go first. Many times the followers in life simply need to be given an opportunity to lead."

Looking at the others, she continued, "While it may have seemed harsh I treated her the way I did, believe me, it was just what she needed. And, don't worry, girls, your turn is coming, so be ready. I'll hurt your feelings and make you uncomfortable before you leave here. That's what the employers pay me to do."

They continued eating and Subira said, "Lola, tell us what you learned today."

Lola put her fork on the plate and dropped her hands to her lap, then said, "Inside I was angry at the way you treated me. Even when I came to dinner, I was still angry. You're right about me wanting to be first. I've never thought about it before, but I guess it's the way I've always been.

"I know Maya is here because of me. I'm not afraid of new things or being someone who leads the way. But, I suppose if a person leads, they're taking responsibility for those who follow. That's a little scary if I think about it. I'd feel horrible if I was responsible for leading Maya into something bad."

Then continuing with a smile, "I suppose the right thing for me to say right now is, 'Thanks Subira for the hard lesson today.'"

The maid removed the dishes from the table while the conversation continued. Then, as the dessert was placed in front of the girls, Subira said, "Hana, let's talk a little bit about what you enjoy in life. What can you tell us?"

Zoya, sitting beside Hana, held her hand under the table. Zoya squeezed it and Hana quietly said, "I suppose what I really like is my family. But I'm feeling guilty because I'm angry with my parents for sending me here. I know they want what's best for me, but right now I'm not seeing this as being a good thing."

Subira responded, "I think before we're done with our two weeks together, you'll see some good things happening. But, can you tell us what you really enjoyed during the last couple of years?"

A first-time smile gradually crept to her lips as she said, "When the moms in our village worked in the fields, I was one of the girls taking care of their babies and kids. I really enjoyed that."

"Well, that's a special thing to do. I think that tells us something about your heart."

Finished with their desserts, Subira said, "We'll start with breakfast at 7:30 a.m. so you can go upstairs and get some rest."

As the girls left the table, Makda lingered and said, "Subira, could we talk?"

"Of course, let's go to the veranda."

Sitting down on the soft chairs, Makda began, "You've treated us very well and I'm thankful for the time you're pouring into us. So, I hesitate in even talking about something, but feel I have to."

"Go ahead Makda. I doubt it'll be something I've not heard before."

"This afternoon I asked you some questions about the traffickers of children and I know I pressed you pretty hard, but now I want to explain something. I'm the oldest of these girls and I've probably seen more about life than they have. So, forgive me and I don't want to appear skeptical or ungrateful, but this evening Mariam asked me a question.

"She said you knew the man who brought her to your home. But, you said earlier today that though you take in trafficked children you do what you can to turn the traffickers over to the authorities. If you already knew Tebeb, then he's probably brought children to you before and yet he's still involved in bringing you kids. I'm not sure I understand."

Subira looked at Makda and said, "You do have questions. I think it's one of your gifts. Many times skepticism can be a weakness because it's an indication of not trusting. But, with you, I think your skepticism is all about caring for these girls. That's a strength.

"Yes, I know Tebeb. I've known him for two years as he's brought many young girls to me. But, all of those girls in the past were sent here by their parents who merely used Tebeb in getting them to Addis. After Tebeb brought Mariam and then left, she told me she'd been taken by force and he'd treated her badly.

"After Mariam told me of her kidnapping, I contacted my friend on the police force and gave him Tebeb's phone number. I'm guessing he's already in custody and won't be doing this again. Unfortunately, it looks like Tebeb's changed. At the beginning, the girls were sent by their parents and he helped us. This is the first time he's crossed the line into kidnapping and that's horrible. He'll pay dearly for that and I doubt he'll be cooperative with the police. That will make it nearly impossible to find out where Mariam came from, but we'll keep trying."

Makda smiled and said, "I knew there'd be an explanation. My pastor told me once that a fountain can't put out both bitter and sweet water at the same time. It'll always be one or the other. You've been very good to us and I'm really thankful you're preparing us for what's next. I thought you'd have an answer. Thanks."

"I'm really happy to help you girls. I wish someone had been there for me when I was in your shoes. Now, it's my turn to do what's right." Then she said, "Makda, you'd better get some rest. Tomorrow will be a big day."

Makda went upstairs and knocked on Mariam's door. Shortly the door opened and Mariam smiled as she saw her new friends face.

"Mariam, I talked to Subira about you and Tebeb. She said she's known him for two years and this is the first time he's taken a girl against her will. She called the police when she found out how you'd been taken. It looks like everything is okay. Does that make you feel better?"

The smile on Mariam's face revealed the answer. "Yes, that helps a lot. Do you think we can trust Subira?"

"Yes. I think we can, but we'll keep our eyes open. She's going to try to get you back home to your family. Now, you go get some rest, okay?" With a hug, she said, "Good night."

Makda closed the door and left.

Chapter 7

Addis Ababa, Ethiopia – Subira's Home
Tuesday, September 8, 2015

MAYA woke early. Maybe it was the birds in the nearby trees or possibly the first rays of dawn on a new day that stirred her. In any case, she laid there and simply enjoyed the soft bed and pillow. Looking around the room she felt happy. Though missing her family, she was feeling some excitement for her future.

Subira seemed a lot like Maya's mom, Faizah, in being direct and in-charge. Maya's personality had seemed more like her dad who was always careful and detailed. He was the one who kept track of their family's coffee plants and their output. He monitored the new plantings and the days of harvest. He watched the weather and knew when to take a day off and when to work longer days. She always admired his attention to the little things.

As she relaxed, she wondered what her day would be like. Yesterday was difficult and she'd felt sad for Lola, but it seemed to end well. Maya had always valued Lola's leadership but there were times when she'd felt frustrated by always being a follower and letting Lola be at the forefront. She'd always thought following others was a gift. Maybe it was and maybe it wasn't. Possibly over the next several days she'd learn to become more assertive.

She reluctantly got out of bed and got dressed for the new day.

Arriving downstairs she went outside and found Makda, Zoya and Hana admiring flowers. Soon the maid called them to breakfast.

Maya looked at the food in front of her. Scrambled eggs, bread, juices and fruit. She wondered if this was an indication of what the rest of her life would be like.

Sitting beside Lola, she waited for Subira to pass the eggs. Before that happened, Maya saw Makda bow her head, shut her eyes and pray. Then, Zoya and Hana did the same.

Subira picked up a platter covered with various breads, passed it to Lola and said, "Girls, after breakfast, we'll go to the courtyard and talk. In the meantime, I wanted to share a few things."

She said, "On Monday, September 21st, you'll be leaving here. I don't know of any other training facilities in Addis just like mine. Normally, young people searching for employment are taken directly to their jobs in the textile mills, factories or to the families for whom they'll do domestic work. I'm what you call a middle-man, or rather, middle-woman, because I offer specialized training to a few young women. I get paid for what I do because I add value to the girls. It's easier and more economical for the factories or families to have me train girls before they arrive at their front doors. By coming through my training, the girl's learning curve happens here rather than in their workplaces. The factory owners and families save money because my girls hit the ground running on their first day.

"I already have some ideas where each of you will be going, but I won't fully decide until two days before you leave. In the meantime, you'll be learning a lot about who you are, your personalities, how to work efficiently, how to care for yourselves, and how to serve others. With this training you'll get the best jobs. Now, let's finish breakfast."

The first two days of training had passed quickly and the evening meal was over. Lying on her bed, Makda thought about the day. Subira did have a real skill in getting the girls to talk about themselves, revealing more of where they'd come from and their hopes and dreams for their future.

The days had been emotionally draining. In many respects, Makda felt sadness for the girls. Most of them had come to Addis unwillingly and their transition wasn't going to be easy. It was like the younger girls were holding onto a life preserver in the open sea trying to keep from drowning. Makda knew it was just a matter of days before the girls would have to let go of the preserver and swim on their own. She knew when that happened it wouldn't be a pretty sight, but it had to happen sooner rather than later.

There was a quiet knock on her door.

"Yes?"

She recognized Hana's voice, "Makda, we're having some soda and cookies if you want to join us?"

"I'll be right there."

There had been something pressing on her mind and she wondered if now was the time to consider doing it. She'd wait to see how the next few minutes went.

The girls had an empty spot on the sofa between Lola and Maya so she tucked her feet under her and settled in.

"So, what are you girls talking about?"

Surprisingly, Mariam said, "We were talking about you."

The rest of the girls giggled.

With a smile Makda replied, "Ah, that's the reason you wanted me out here. You were feeling guilty talking about me behind my back?"

They laughed again.

Zoya said, "No, we were trying to understand something. You had said you wanted to go to Riyadh, Saudi Arabia. That seems like a long way from here. Why would you want to go there when you could stay here in Addis and do the same thing?"

Before Makda could answer, Lola blurted, "What language do they speak there? I doubt it's Amharic or Oromo like we have here."

Hana said, "It's Saudi Arabian language."

Makda replied, "Actually it's called Arabic."

"So you'll need to learn Arabic?"

"I guess so. Actually I think it'll be kind of easy since I'll be living with a family and learning it every day. Unless I learn their language I'll have no one to talk to."

Maya asked, "So, why are you going to Saudi Arabia?"

Makda was cautious. Maya, Lola and Mariam were Muslim but she knew God was opening this door. She willingly went through it.

"Because it's an answer to one of my prayers."

Hana asked, "What prayer?"

"Three years ago, my pastor told us about a prayer we should consider praying. Do you girls want to know about it?"

Prayer was one thing all the girls had in common so there was a unanimous 'yes'.

"Okay. Let me get my Book and I'll read the prayer to you."

In her room she picked up her Bible and then pulled a box from her dresser drawer. Opening it, she took out five small Bibles and returned to the girls.

She found 1 Chronicles chapter 4, gave a Bible and a pen to each of the girls and told them the page number. Finally, each one found the page.

Makda said, "Go down to verse 10 and I'll read it to you."

"Lord, bless me. Expand my borders and coasts. Put your hands on me and keep me from evil so I won't experience grief."

She looked at the girls and said, "Underline the prayer so it'll be easier to find. I've prayed that prayer every day for the last three years and I've been waiting for God to show me what He wanted me to do. Then it happened!"

Lola, with excitement asked, "What? What happened?"

"Well, you know I lost my mom and dad in an accident but I was able to keep our home. Then I found out the city was going to tear down a lot of homes in our neighborhood, including mine, to make way for apartment buildings. I knew I'd have to move. Then, a day or so later, I was at a bus stop, sitting on a bench and feeling really sad about losing my home. Beside me on the bench was a brochure, so I picked it up and read it."

"What did it say?"

"It said, *'Travel Abroad – Employment Opportunities in Exotic Riyadh'*. I knew right then God was answering my prayers. He was going to expand my borders and coasts and I knew what I needed to do! I made an appointment for an interview, was accepted and now I'm here.

"I knew I had to be obedient to what God was asking me to do. To be honest, I don't want to leave Ethiopia. Everything here is familiar to me, the food, language and culture. This is where my friends are. Everything, and I mean everything will be different in Saudi Arabia. Honestly, I'm scared, but I know I have to do this for God."

Maya asked, "Why would Allah want you in Saudi Arabia when he could use you here?"

Makda replied, "That's a really good question and I don't have the answer for it. Talk to me in five years. Maybe then I'll know."

Continuing, she held her Bible in her hands and said, "You can keep the Book I gave you if you want to since you've just underlined some things in it."

Maya replied, "You know Lola and I are Muslim, don't you?"

"Yes, the two of you and Mariam too."

Maya continued, "I once asked my dad a question. I asked him if there was a difference between our Muslim Quran, the Jewish Torah and Psalms, and the Christian Bible. He told me that 'Allah gave the Quran to the prophet Muhammad; the Koran to the prophet Moses; the Psalms to the prophet David; and the Bible to the prophet Jesus.'"

Then she continued, "Dad told me he considers all the books good, but the Quran is the final and unchanged word of Allah."

Makda asked again, "Would you like to keep the book?"

Maya briefly looked at Lola and then said, "I'll take it. Thanks."

Lola and Mariam kept theirs as well.

Makda said, "There's more good teachings in this Book. Maybe over the next few days we can look at some more together."

Kamali admired her boss's ability to mold and shape people. She said, "Subira, it seems the girls are getting along really well together."

The two were sitting on the veranda and enjoying a late evening chai. They heard the bedroom doors close upstairs and knew the girls were done for the day.

Subira replied, "Yes, but it isn't always that way, is it?"

"No, this seems to be a special group."

"Kamali, what do you think? Do you see any problems?"

"You'd know better than I would, but I've not seen anything that concerns me. How about you?"

Subira answered, "Makda's a bright girl with a sensitive spirit and heart. With some of our previous trainees we had to watch them so they weren't cruel to each other. Makda's the opposite. I think she'd do anything for these girls even if it hurt herself. Makda's good heart could do some damage though. We'll have to keep an eye on her."

"How do you think she could do damage?"

Subira looked at Kamali and said, "By asking too many questions. I think I have her in a safe spot for now, but it doesn't take much to stir the skepticism in her. When she starts asking questions, it could cause the others to ask questions too."

Kamali said, "The other girls seem to respect her and I can understand why. She's really kind and sweet, but I'll keep watching her."

She continued, "I wondered what you were thinking about Hana. She doesn't seem to connect with the other girls. Are you concerned?"

"Even though I think Hana is the most vulnerable, I think she'll be just fine. In some respects she and Mariam are similar, except Mariam is only nine and quickly connected with Makda. That'll be an attachment that'll help Mariam a lot. Though Zoya and Hana have connected, there's only three years difference between them. They're more like peers so there won't be a deep connection in the short time they're with us."

Subira turned to Kamali and quietly said, "If the girls had any idea what was ahead of them, we'd likely lose them all. What they're experiencing right now are probably the best days of their lives. Getting out into the real world isn't a smooth transition. It'll be tough for them. It always is.

"I've got six agents coming on the 21st to take the girls to their jobs. I have a pretty good idea of where they'll be going but we still have some time to fine tune everything. We want to be certain the jobs fit the girls."

Kamali asked, "You want to give me some hints of what you're thinking?"

"No, not yet. In fact, I'd like you to be thinking about where you'd place them. You sit in on all the training sessions, so let's see what you'd do. Maybe you'll have a good idea in five days or so?"

"Okay. I'll give it a try."

"Well, it's getting late. I'm going to bed. Good night Kamali."

Chapter 8

Addis Ababa, Ethiopia – Subira's Home
Monday, September 14, 2015

***"DID** you see that?"*

Maya looked at Lola and asked, "What?"

"That man lying on the ground over there! I think he's a beggar. He doesn't have hardly any clothes on and he's really dirty!"

Overhearing, Kamali said, "Lola, he's a leper. Here in Addis, there are thousands of them. They're probably the poorest of the poor. If a person gets leprosy, the whole family is shunned, making it really difficult for any of them to get jobs. Most turn to begging for a few birr here at the market." Then she said, "Lola and Maya, come with me."

Kamali went toward the man with the girls reluctantly following. Kamali retrieved a few coins from her purse and gave them to the girls and said, "Go ahead. Give him the coins. He won't hurt you."

Maya hung back as Lola approached the man. He held out his hand and she gently placed two coins into a fingerless palm. Maya followed and did the same.

Lola exclaimed, "Did you see that? He didn't have any fingers on his right hand and only two on his left!"

Maya said, "And some of his toes were missing."

Kamali said, "Sometimes the leprosy affects their ears and nose too. Some lose their eyesight. It's a horrible disease. About 4,000 new cases are diagnosed every year in Ethiopia."

Earlier that morning at breakfast, Subira had said, "Girls, today we're going to do something unusual. The last three days have been busy, so today we're going to the Mercato Market. It'll be part of your training.

"Mercato is huge and you can buy literally anything you'd want there... if you have the money! So, Mariam, you'll go with Makda and the rest of you will do some shopping on your own. I'll give each of you a list of items we need as well as the money to buy it. There'll be money left over so I want you to find a coffee shop and get yourself something to drink. I'll be giving you two hours to get it all done."

Zoya had asked, "But, we don't know our way around. Won't we get lost?"

Subira laughed and said, "When we get there, I'll give you some boundaries and instructions and you'll get along just fine."

Zoya said, "We don't have watches and you're setting a time limit. How will we know when it's time to meet you?"

Again, Subira laughed and said, "When you're finished with your training and leave my home, you'll find out you need to learn how to 'make do'. I'm sure when you're in the market you'll figure out a way to find your way to me on time."

Walking with Kamali, Lola looked back at the man with leprosy. She couldn't help but feel sympathy for him and wondered if he had a wife and children.

They joined Subira and the other girls. They were busy looking at large wicker baskets filled to the brim with many different spices and seeds. The smell under the tent was intense but not unpleasant.

Zoya said, "I'd guess nothing has changed here for 200 years. The smells and sounds are probably still the same."

Mariam, usually quiet, said, "The smells remind me of my mom's cooking."

Subira said, "Mariam, remember what I said a few days ago? We're going to speak about the future, not the past. Okay?"

Mariam submissively said, "Yes ma'am."

"All right girls, follow me. I'm going to take you to our meeting place. There are many, many streets and alleys in Mercato and it's an easy place to get lost. Always know where you came from, where you're at and where you're going. That's important."

She pointed to a spindly tower. The girls shaded their eyes from the hot early afternoon sun to see a tall, thin minaret indicating a Muslim mosque. "Girls, that's your landmark."

Subira said, "We're going to meet right here in about two hours. The muezzin climbs the minaret and stands on his small porch and invites the Muslims to prayer five times a day. At dawn, noon, mid-afternoon, sunset and night. When he calls for the mid-afternoon prayers, we'll see you right here. So, no matter where you go from here, look for the minaret, listen for the muezzin and you'll be just fine."

Kamali gave each of the girls money and a list of items to purchase.

Subira said, "Girls, this is your chance. You have two hours on your own and responsibility to get a job done. Stay focused on what you need to do. There's an old proverb that says, *'You must attend to your business with the market vendor and not to the noise of the market.'*"

"Okay. I'll see you here when the muezzin begins the call to prayer."

Hana watched as Zoya, Lola and Maya headed in various directions, Makda and Mariam in another. She saw Subira and Kamali sitting down in an outdoor café.

She felt alone and almost frozen in fear. How could she do this? Then she thought about helping the injured Abena on their three mile hike from the volcano to her home. Smiling, she thought, 'I can do this'.

Looking at her list, she didn't know where to start. Seeing the word *'berbere'* among the items, she headed to the tent where the group had looked at spices.

Ducking her head under a flapping piece of canvas, she looked at the various spices. Her mom used berbere spice for their stews and sauces back in Ropi. She felt guilty thinking about the past, but she knew her mind was hers to do with as she wanted. Then she smelled the berbere before she saw it. Its color was something between red and orange. She knew it was made of chili, peppers, ginger, garlic and another half-dozen spices. She paid the woman for a bag of the spice and soon was back on the street. Looking at her list she saw the next item, 'six bars of soap'.

Looking right, then left, she didn't know where to go. Then, suddenly she felt a twinge of fear. Where was the minaret? Already she'd failed to keep track of where she'd been and where she was going. Walking to an intersection she looked all around and finally saw the tower. Relieved, she again looked for a soap vendor. Perplexed, she went back to the spice vendor and simply asked the woman. She took Hana outside and pointed to a vendor a half block up the street. With a quick thanks, Hana hurried to the spot.

Walking in, she was amazed at all the varieties of soap. Grabbing six home-made bars from a pile, she paid for them.

Back on the street, she looked at the third and last item. Figs. Realizing it was better to ask questions than to search on her own, she went back into the soap tent and asked the woman for a location to purchase the figs.

Again, the vendor took her outside the tent and gave directions. The fig location would be more difficult because it was four streets away. Thanking the woman, she looked up, located the minaret and headed to the fruit market.

Purchasing the figs, she knew there was only one thing left to do. She needed to find a café and purchase something to drink. Hana didn't understand why it was necessary, but she had the time and the money. So, she walked down the street.

Noticing two café's nearby, she wondered which one she should enter. Then, she remembered the one near the minaret. Realizing if she went to that café now, she wouldn't have to worry about finding the minaret later and risk being late.

Retracing her steps to the soap seller and the spice vendor, she saw the minaret. Looking down the street she saw the café and walked toward it. Going inside, she stood in a line wondering what she should order. Remembering a special coffee she had at Subira's, her decision was made. She approached the girl behind the counter and ordered a 'macchiato'. She watched as the girl whipped up the hot milk, chocolate drizzle and coffee.

The girl brought the steaming hot coffee to Hana and said, "You're pretty young to be drinking this. How old are you?"

Suddenly her confidence waned and she felt vulnerable. She quietly answered, "I'm thirteen."

"Oh, I'm teasing you. I've been drinking coffee since I was six years old."

Paying for the macchiato, she went outside to a small table and sat down.

She relaxed in the warm sunshine and smiled. She'd fulfilled her responsibilities with time and money to spare. The minaret was less than a minutes' walk away. Success!

She sipped the hot and sweet macchiato and watched the people on the street, at the vendor's booths and at the other café tables. A young woman sitting at another table smiled at her. Hana returned the smile. The woman stood, clutching her coffee and approached Hana. "May I join you?"

Hana didn't know what to do, other than to say, "Okay."

The beautiful young woman sat down and said, "My name is Halima."

Hana looked at her and replied, "My name is Hana."

"Hana. That's a pretty name. I think it's in the Bible. Are you Protestant?"

"Yes, I am. My parents named me after the Hana of the Old Testament."

"I'm Protestant too. How old are you Hana?"

"I'm thirteen."

"Were you born in Addis?"

"No, I come from Ropi."

"I don't know where that's at. How did you find your way here?"

Hana told her a quick version of the last week's travels and experiences.

When she was done, Halima quietly said, "I saw you earlier with the other girls." Pausing, she said, "I know Subira."

Wide-eyed, Hana looked at Halima and asked, "You know her?"

"Yes."

"How do you know her?"

Halima said quietly and with sincerity, "Hana, I'm going to tell you something and I want you to listen carefully to what I have to say."

Hana felt a fear gripping her stomach and waited for what was to come.

"I grew up in Addis Ababa and my dad helped me get into Subira's program four years ago when I was fifteen. I went through her two week training program and learned a lot. But I've learned a lot more since then. I know what you're going through, but more importantly I know what's ahead of you because I've now lived it.

"I was in this market four years ago, just like you, buying things as part of our training. There were six of us. It seems so long ago.

"Listen to me. You need to get away from Subira. Did she say when you'd be leaving her home?"

Hana, now feeling confused said, "We're leaving in a week. I think it's on Monday, the 21st. Why?"

"Is this your first trip to Mercato or your second?"

"This is the first time I've been here."

"Hana, Subira is going to literally sell you to someone on the 21st. I don't know who it'll be, but trust me, no good will come from it. The person she'll be selling you to will use you in a factory, in a home or on the streets. And, believe me, you don't want to live like that. None of it will be good."

Now angry, Hana said, "Halima, I don't know you, but I know Subira. She and Kamila have been very kind to us and I've never had it so nice. I can't believe Subira would want any harm to come to any of us. In fact, she's given us two hours on our own here at Mercato. She even gave us money. I'm not sure I can believe what you're saying!"

Halima patiently and quietly responded, "Don't you understand? That's exactly what she wants you to believe. It's exactly how it went for me. But now, even after four years, I don't have enough money to leave the horrible life she sold me into. I have to do things I don't want to talk about, to simply make enough money to survive. The man I was with this afternoon bought me this coffee because I didn't have enough money to buy my own. I've been beaten several times and stabbed once because of the work Subira sold me into. That's the truth.

"Some of the girls get good jobs. Others are sold for a lot more money for not-so-good work. Subira isn't who she seems to be."

Doubtful, Hana shook her head and said, "Well, I still can't believe it's true."

"Okay. I understand. I'm a total stranger. If I were in your shoes, I don't think I'd believe a stranger either. But I'm telling you that what I say is true." Then pausing, she said with desperation, "Let me prove it to you."

"How can you do that?"

Halima said, "I can predict what'll happen next. If I'm right, then maybe you'll believe me. Tonight, she'll ask each of you to answer five questions.

"'Did you feel any fear today?'
'What was the best part of your two hours?'
'What did you get at the café?'
'What was the café's name?'

And the last question will be, 'Did you talk to anyone interesting?'"

She continued, "Then, two days from now, on Wednesday, Kamali will take you girls in the car and drop you off individually at different locations around the city. You'll have four hours to find your way back. She'll give you Subira's address in case you get lost, but you're not to use it unless you're desperate.

"Next Thursday, she's going to take you to a clinic for an exam.

"On Friday, at breakfast, Subira will tell you girls you're going back to Mercato for another day out of the house. She'll give you more money and another list. Only this time she'll give you just an hour to get it done. I'm guessing today you had two hours?"

Hesitantly, Hana said, "Yes, two hours."

"Okay. I know you're not believing me and I don't blame you. But, if all the things I've just told you are right, then you're going to want to listen to me and get away from Subira. I'll be here in this café next Friday morning. If you want me to help you get away, make sure you've brought your things with you and meet me right here. Don't buy anything on your list but come directly here. Do you understand?"

"Yes, I understand. But I don't think you'll see me again."

With a threatening glare, Hana continued, "What would Subira say if I told her tonight I had met you at this café? What would she say about all the things you've said about her? What if I told her you wanted to help me get away from her?"

Halima, now with fear in her eyes, looked at Hana and said, "Trust me. Don't tell her or the other girls about us talking. That wouldn't be good for you and it really wouldn't be good for me. If you're having a tough time believing me, I'm sure the other girls would be even more doubtful. If you don't want to meet me next Friday, I understand. I'm just trying to help you. I only wish someone had been here to help me four years ago."

Then, the muezzin began his call to prayer for the Muslim faithful. The loudspeakers were blaring the chanting which settled over the Mercato marketplace. Halima smiled and looked directly at Hana. She said, "If I remember right, that's your signal to meet Subira. Am I right?"

Hana, stunned at Halima's knowledge, simply got up and entered the street. She didn't look back.

The girls were giggling and chattering about their time in the market as they approached the van. Hana quietly listened and watched as they spoke of their experiences at Mercato.

Twenty minutes later they arrived at the home and Subira said, "Dinner will be at six. We'll see you at the table then."

Hana retreated to her room and laid on her bed. Looking around at her surroundings, she couldn't believe Subira was evil. If she were, would she let her trainees live in a place like this? Would she have provided two hours of freedom this afternoon? Would she have entrusted her with money?

It became clear to her then. There were only two possible answers. Either Halima was a liar for some unknown reason, or Subira was a liar and absolutely the best actress in the world. Right now she saw no reason to not trust Subira and Kamali.

Then she remembered her dad. Raised as a Protestant, he always went to His Bible when he was struggling with questions. Hana reached over and retrieved the small Bible which Makda had given her. She prayed, 'Lord, I have more questions than answers. Help me, please! In Jesus' name, Amen'.

Then she opened the Bible and began reading. Though she read nothing that gave her any answers to the riddle before her, she felt a connection to God and her dad.

She was still nowhere closer to finding an answer to her dilemma, but at least she felt peaceful as she descended the staircase to the first floor.

Subira wasn't one to waste precious time, so she started asking questions during dinner.

"Maya, did you enjoy your time at Mercato?"

"Yes, but I'm sorry I wasn't able to find the Kosoret spice on my list. I went to five spice vendors and none of them had any."

"That's okay. I know you tried. Tell me, was there anything that happened today that made you fearful?"

Immediately Hana tensed. That was the first question Halima had said would be asked!

Maya said, "I was afraid you'd be unhappy with me for not finding the Kosoret."

Kindly, Subira responded, "It's obvious you tried. But, to survive, you'll need to become more resourceful. Did you ask anyone in the market for help in finding the spice?"

Maya hung her head and said, "No."

Again, Subira gently said, "Well, there you go. I'd bet next time you'll know what to do. In fact, you'll get another chance on Saturday, because we're going to do it again."

Hana laid down her fork and placed her trembling hands on her lap. She'd just heard another point of Halima's prophecy coming true. But Halima had said the trip would be Friday instead of Saturday.

Hana tentatively interrupted Subira, "Did you say Saturday?"

Quizzically Subira looked at Hana. "Oh my, you are the observant one. I did say Saturday, but actually it'll be Friday. My mistake."

Then Subira asked, "Hana, what made you question the day? I don't recall saying anything about going back to the market?"

Hana, realizing her blunder, hesitated and then replied, "I just wondered what we'll be doing the rest of the week?"

Subira responded, "No matter, let's keep going or it'll get late."

"Maya, what was the best part of your time in the market?"

"Oh, finding all of you and being finished!"

"And the worst?"

Maya hesitated and then said, "Actually, not having enough time to get to the café and missing out on my coffee."

"Well, it seems like you learned quite a lot this afternoon! Were you able to talk to anyone interesting during your time at Mercato?"

Maya, obviously embarrassed, said, "One of the women at a spice booth said I should be in the movies since... "

"Since what, Maya?"

Hesitating, and looking down she whispered, "... since I'm so beautiful."

"Oh, now that's interesting! I'd have to agree with the spice vendor. Maya, you're a very beautiful girl."

Hana realized all of Halima's questions were asked in one form or another. Those facts at least proved Halima probably knew Subira and had been a part of Subira's 'family'. But, it didn't prove Subira had evil intent.

"Mariam. You and Makda spent your time at the market together. Was there ever a time you felt fear this afternoon?"

Mariam looked at Makda and began, "No, since I was with Makda, everything... "

Hana's mind began to drift into confusion and fear as each of the girls answered Subira's questions.

Then she heard, "Hana. How about you? Was there any time you felt fear today?"

Hana forced her mind back to the discussion. "Yes, one time. I was so intent on finding the items on the list I forgot to keep track of where the mosque minaret was."

Subira asked, "That would've been scary. Obviously you found it. What was your best time today?"

"Oh, pretty simple. When I finally saw the minaret again."

"Kamali said you got all your items on the list. That's great! So, were you able to go to a café?"

"Yes."

"Good. What was its name?"

Hana replied, "It was called Somali Coast Café.

"I know that café. What did you get?"

"I got a macchiato."

"Were you able to talk to anyone interesting during your time at the market?"

Hana silently looked at Subira and then at her unfinished dessert.

"Hana?"

Her mind in turmoil, she responded, "Yes. At the café a girl..."

Hana hesitated.

"Yes Hana? What about a girl?"

Hana looked at Subira again and said, "... a girl behind the counter asked me how old I was. When I told her I was thirteen, she said I was too young to be drinking coffee. Then she told me she began drinking it when she was only six years old." Pausing, she continued, "I guess I found it interesting someone would tell me I was too young when she was only six when she started."

Subira laughed as some of the girls giggled. "Thanks Hana for sharing. Now let's get our desserts finished and then you can all relax until bedtime."

When they arrived upstairs, Makda told the girls, "If you want, bring your Books and I'll show you something special."

Makda wasn't sure if all the girls would join her. She was thankful to see all five bringing their Bibles.

"We're only going to be together for another week, so I want to give you some new verses to underline in your Book. Turn to page 63. That's the book of the prophet Isaiah. In chapter 43, the second verse is really special to me. It tells me that when I am passing through the waters and rivers, God will be with me and the rivers won't flow over me. It also says that when I'm walking through fire, I won't be burned and the flame won't harm me.

"I want you to underline that verse because it's a promise you'll probably need someday.

"Now turn back two pages. In the prophet Isaiah, chapter 41, verse ten, it tells us we shouldn't fear because God is with us. He says we shouldn't be discouraged because He's our God. He promises to give us strength and help when we're weak and He'll hold us up with His right hand. Underline that verse too.

"There's just one more verse to look at. Go forward four pages to chapter 49, verse 16. The Lord says He's engraved or tattooed our names on the palms of His hands.

Lola asked, "Why would He do that?"

Zoya said, "Is it because He loves us so much and He wants us to know He'll never forget us?"

Makda responded, "I think that's exactly why He'd want to have our names on His hands."

Mariam laughed and said, "I had no idea Allah's hands were big enough to hold all our names!"

"It's hard to imagine, but the book of Psalms, chapter 95, verse four tells us God is able to hold the deepest places of the earth in His hand. If He's able to do that, then I'm sure He's able to take care of a nine-year-old girl from the desert!"

Makda closed her Bible and said, "Okay girls, time for bed. See you at breakfast."

The next day was filled with learning life skills. Subira had said, "No matter what you'll do in life and no matter where you'll live, these lessons are things you can use the rest of your lives."

Together they learned the basics of health care, nutrition, first aid, and accounting.

On Wednesday morning, Subira said, "Girls, today you're going to do something unusual. Kamali will be dropping each of you off in different parts of Addis and you'll need to find your way back to my home. Mariam will go with Makda but the rest of you are on your own. As you leave with Kamali, make sure you look for landmarks or things in the neighborhood that will help you get home. I also want you to remember our home is between the Somalian Embassy and the Congolese Embassy. That will get you close. Use your brains to find your way home. You'll have four hours to get back. Any questions?"

Zoya asked, "What if we get lost and can't find our way back?"

Kamali answered, "I'll give you the address for our home. I don't want you to use it unless you won't be able to get home otherwise."

Subira looked at the girls and stopped as she noticed Hana's face. With what seemed to be an inquisitive look, she asked, "Hana. Are you okay? Is something the matter?"

Hana had grown increasingly fearful as Subira outlined the plans for the day. The fear came from the growing realization that Halima's list of predictions of what was coming next was rapidly being fulfilled.

"Hana? Are you okay?"

"Yes, ma'am. I'm okay. Being alone on the streets for four hours seems scary. I grew up in a village and Addis seems huge."

Subira smiled reassuringly and said, "You'll be okay. Believe me, you won't be the only thirteen-year-old on the streets of Addis Ababa today!"

All the girls eventually found their way back to Subira's home. At dinner, each shared their experience. Most had been overwhelmed at what they saw of life in the capital city.

Zoya, while walking, had been threatened by two large dogs. A man in a truck saw what was happening and chased the dogs away. He offered to give Zoya a ride. She'd simply asked him to take her to the neighborhood between the two embassies. He did and she was back home in thirty minutes.

It hadn't gone so well for Maya. After Kamali had dropped her off, she began walking. Finally after two hours, she asked a shop owner for help and found she'd been walking in the wrong direction the entire time. Feeling empathy after hearing her story, he allowed one of his delivery truck drivers to get her to the neighborhood. She arrived home an hour early.

Lola was the only one who had walked the entire way. She'd asked for directions to the Congolese Embassy. Stubbornly, she refused to ask for a ride. She was five minutes late, but thrilled to tell the others about her 'hike'.

Makda and Mariam reluctantly said they had to give Subira's address to a woman so they could find their way back. Makda said, "Following directions has never been my talent. I'm the oldest and the only one who had to use the address. Now, that's pretty sad!" Looking at Mariam, she smiled and said, "You'll need to go with someone else next time!"

Hana had walked for two hours until she remembered she had left-over birr from her Mercato Market shopping experience. She took a taxi to the Congolese Embassy, paid her fare and asked an embassy guard for directions to the Somalian Embassy. Walking the few streets between them she easily found the home an hour early.

Subira said, "Whether you made it on time, had to use the address or whatever else you had to do, you've used the resources you had to accomplish the task. I'm impressed! You girls are survivors."

The next day, as Halima had predicted, the girls went to a clinic for a medical examination. Subira had said, "Your employers want to be assured you're healthy and capable of doing your jobs. The doctor will be giving you a certificate we can give to your new employer. It'll be very valuable to your employer as they only want healthy people."

Evenings were special as Makda continued to highlight special Bible verses for the girls.

On Thursday evening, she showed them the first three chapters of St. John.

She said, "The verses I've shared with you the other nights are all really important. They're verses that'll help you get through tough days. But the verses in St. John will help you get through a tough life."

Zoya agreed and said, "Makda's right. No matter who we are, where we've come from or where we're going, these three chapters are life-changing."

Maya asked, "Who wrote these chapters?"

Makda replied, "A man named John. He was a follower of Jesus and wrote about the things Jesus said and did."

Maya pressed, "So, how do we know his words are true?"

Zoya said, "I know they're true because when I accepted them and made them a part of my life, my life changed forever."

Makda said, "Each of you will have the rest of your lives to read these words again and again. I know they'll become personal to you and then you'll know their truth just like Zoya and I."

Chapter 9

Addis Ababa, Ethiopia – Subira's Home
Friday, September 18, 2015

HANA'S eyes adjusted to the darkness of her bedroom. It had taken her a while to get to sleep but now she was wide awoke. The house was quiet, dark and made her wonder what time it was.

Quietly she got out of bed and went to the window. Pushing aside the cloth curtain she knelt by the open window and stared out into the darkness. She heard a dog barking and almost simultaneously a rooster crowed. She smiled, wondering if the rooster was also having difficulty sleeping. Dawn was hours away.

Turning on the small lamp by her bedside, she reached for her Bible. Her mom had told her a few years ago about a couple of verses that had meant a lot to her. Thinking of her mom brought a momentary melancholy which she dismissed quickly by opening the Bible. She remembered the verses were in the Gospel of John.

She finally found what she was looking for. The message seemed to be coming from her mother as she read verses 31, 32 and 36 in chapter 8.

'If you abide in my word, you are my disciples indeed. And you shall know the truth, and the truth shall make you free. Therefore if the Son makes you free, you shall be free indeed.'

Hana closed the Bible and turned off the light. Covered by a sheet and lying on a soft pillow in a safe and comfortable house made her feel secure. Then she wondered what would happen on Monday. What if Halima was right? What if Subira would sell her to someone who was cruel? What if Subira was, in reality, an evil woman? What if all she'd experienced in the last ten days was just a charade?

But, what if Halima wasn't right? Was there a chance Halima had her own evil intentions? If only her mom and dad were here to give her advice and answers. She desperately wanted help in making the right decision, but her frustration was growing just as fast as her confusion.

In some respects the Bible verses from St. John did give her insight. There was the promise that if she continued reading God's Word and following Jesus, she'd find truth.

The confusion was coming from the fact that the actions of Subira were seemingly kind. Yet, at the same time, Halima seemed to have no ulterior motives. She remembered her dad quoting a Bible verse about 'wolves dressed in sheep's wool'. Who's the wolf and who's the sheep? She prayed God would reveal truth to her before she made a wrong decision.

As she awoke at dawn she once again heard a crowing rooster and barking dog. A bathroom door was shutting in the hallway and jolted Hana to the reality of another day. Today was Friday. Another day closer to Monday. This would be the day the girls would go back to Mercato Market and she could meet with Halima if she chose to.

A few days from now Subira would transfer her to her employer. Or, if Halima was correct, Monday would be the day Hana would come face to face with evil. Today was the only chance she'd have to make a choice. She could continue to believe in Subira's promises or she could choose to believe Halima's accusations against Subira.

She got dressed, uttered another prayer and looked around the room. Halima had told her to bring her belongings to the market. Hana, though she hadn't decided what to do as yet, did decide to take what she could. Grabbing her Bible, a few small personal items and a couple of articles of clothing, she pushed them into a small backpack which she placed behind her bed. She descended the staircase and joined the others at breakfast.

Subira said, "Well, here she is! Good morning Hana. You get the award for sleeping the latest."

The rest of the girls laughed as Hana, obviously embarrassed, hung her head.

"Don't worry. It happens to us all. Now, it's time for breakfast. We have a big day ahead of us!"

As the girls walked to the van for the ride to Mercato, Subira noticed the backpack Hana was carrying and said, "Hana?"

"Yes ma'am?"

"Why are you taking your backpack to the market? You realize you're the only one of the girls doing that?"

Hana quietly said, "If you don't want me to, I'll leave it here." Then she gathered a bit of courage and continued, "Last time I was at Mercato, it wasn't easy carrying all the items through the market. I thought it'd be easier if I had something to carry them in."

Subira looked at Hana and said, "Girls, it seems that Hana is thinking ahead. I like that! Why don't each of you grab your packs and then we'll leave."

The girls returned and piled into the van.

Arriving at the mosque's minaret, the six girls, Subira and Kamali stood on the street.

Kamali said, "Here's your list of items to buy and the money to get it done. There's also enough money for you to get a coffee after you've bought your stuff. Today the muezzin gives his call to the faithful at noon. That's when you need to be here at this spot to leave. Remember, you only have an hour. Let's see how you do."

Hana turned around and watched as the other five girls moved toward the open market. Hana watched as Subira and Kamali walked toward the nearest café. Horrified, she realized it was the café where she was to meet Halima. Then, Hana saw Subira turn and look directly at her. So, reluctantly, she began walking down another street. Now what? Possibly God was 'directing her path'. Maybe God didn't want her to meet with Halima?

She'd been frightened when Subira had asked about her backpack. If she'd looked inside, there would have been no way to answer Subira's questions about the extra clothing, but that didn't happen. Again she wondered... was God giving her a path to take by not having her pack's contents discovered?

She knew she needed to at least meet Halima. Possibly something would happen or be said which would give an indication of what she was to do next.

She kept walking. Halima was nowhere to be found. Hana began to wonder if possibly her decision would be made for her. If Halima didn't come, then she'd have her answer. That would make it easy.

Almost relieved it could be that simple, she sat at a table outside another café and decided to wait a few minutes. Much longer than that would jeopardize her ability to get the items on her list.

She watched the people in the busy market. As she watched two children arguing in the street, someone tapped her shoulder. Turning, Hana saw a young woman she didn't recognize. The woman said, "Are you Hana?"

"Yes, who are you?"

"My name is Amara. Halima sent me."

Quickly sitting down at the table, Amara said, "We don't have much time. I'm a good friend of Halima. She and I were at Subira's together a few years ago. She told me you were having a difficult time believing her so she sent me to talk to you. Everything Halima told you is true and everything that's happening with Subira is a sham. Hana, you need to believe us. Monday, Subira will be moving you on. You'll go to some employer who won't care about you. He'll use you and discard you like a piece of trash. Your only hope is to come with us today and we'll do our very best to take care of you. Will you come?"

Flustered, Hana realized she had to make a decision. Subira could have easily found her clothing in her bag, but she didn't. Amara was correct that she did have a difficult time believing Halima. But, now, having two young women telling her the same thing was mildly convincing.

Hana weighed her options in her twirling mind. Why did it have to be so difficult? Neither option seemed perfect.

She looked directly into Amara's eyes and saw sincerity.

"Where's Halima?"

Amara pointed to a woman on the street corner. "There."

The woman pulled back a scarf and Hana recognized her.

Hana's hands and voice shook with apprehension and fear of the unknown, then she blurted, "Okay. I'll go with you."

Quickly, Amara grabbed Hana's hand and led her to Halima who hugged her.

"I'm so glad you believe us. Now, we'll need to disappear quickly."

Halima pulled a scarf from her bag and draped it around Hana's head and over her mouth. Soon they were several streets away from the minaret and going deeper into the massive market.

Then, Hana saw Makda and Mariam coming out of a vendor's booth. They passed within ten feet of her and Hana noticed both of the girls were laughing. She desperately wanted to reach out to them. Then the doubts overwhelmed her. What if she'd made the wrong decision? *Where are these strangers taking me?*

The trio continued on, oblivious to the thousands of people shopping at Mercato.

Lola heard the muezzin begin the call to prayer and quickly returned to the minaret meeting place. Subira and Kamali were waiting as she arrived with her backpack of produce and bags of flour. Soon, Makda and Mariam arrived, with Zoya and Maya a minute later.

Waiting another five minutes, Subira asked, "Has anyone seen Hana?"

"The last I saw her was when we left here an hour ago," said Maya.

The rest of the girls agreed. Subira looked at Kamali and said, "Check the cafés near here. We'll wait."

Ten minutes later, Kamali returned to the group and shook her head. "I couldn't find her anywhere."

Subira said, "We'll wait another ten minutes and then we'll need to leave. Do any of you girls have any idea what's happening?"

The five girls shook their heads 'no'.

Ten minutes passed and Subira said, "Let's go." Then to Kamali, "You stay in case she shows up. If she's not here within the next two hours, come back to the house."

The girls were quiet on the return trip. Maya asked, "Subira, what do you think happened to her?"

"I don't know. I have no idea."

Zoya said, "I'm worried. She's just a thirteen-year-old country girl in a really big city."

Subira was quiet.

Kamali arrived home almost three hours later, just as the girls were getting seated at the table for dinner.

She said, "Hana never came back. I asked a lot of people about her and no one knew anything which isn't too surprising. Everyone there is focused on what they're buying or selling so they don't pay any attention to others."

Subira said, "Girls, we're going to assume Hana won't be coming back and I know there'll be a disappointed employer on Monday. I'm sure Hana has the address for my home, so she may still show up. We'll hope for the best."

The atmosphere around the dinner table was subdued. Subira went through her usual questions regarding their day and then said, "The day at Mercato went perfect, except for Hana's disappearance. You all purchased your products, had time for coffee and returned to the van on time. I'm impressed. Now, it's been a long day, so why don't you get some rest."

Halima, Amara and Hana had walked through the market and then through a residential area consisting mostly of small, rickety, wooden huts. The huts were like a long continuous wall constructed of wood, plastic and tin with a door every ten or fifteen feet. There were splashes of color here and there, but the predominant colors were black and brown. The road was paved for a few blocks but soon turned into a pot-holed, muddy, narrow street.

Halima turned into a small side alley and approached a wooden door. Retrieving her key, she removed the padlock from the door and stepped inside. Amara and Hana entered.

Hana looked around the single room and saw two small beds, a table and four chairs. The room was neat and clean but tiny. There wasn't a bathroom or kitchen but there were shelves with a few dishes and other miscellaneous items.

Halima looked at Hana and said, "I'm sure you're wondering why you left Subira's place for this. I know this isn't much. But over the next few days, you'll have a better idea about why this is better than if you'd stayed at Subira's until Monday."

Amara continued, "Tomorrow we'll show you around and explain some things to you. When you were at Subira's, not everything was as it seemed. The same is true here."

Halima said, "Hana, we'll go out and get our evening meal and come back here to eat. You'll be safe and I know you'll not be sorry you're here with us."

Going out to the muddy street, the three walked two minutes to a food vendor who was selling injera, sauce and vegetables. Amara paid the woman for the meals and they walked back to the hut.

Seated around the table, they began eating. Hana said, "This food is really good! Maybe it's because I haven't eaten anything since breakfast."

The three talked about many things. Dusk came and Halima lit three candles. "We don't have electricity. A lot of people steal it by splicing into the wires outside, but it's not worth it. If you don't electrocute yourself, you're at risk of getting caught. If you're caught, there's a fine to pay. If you can't pay the fine, it's jail. Believe me, you don't want to go to jail."

Amara said, "Hana, we have a blanket you can put on the floor if you're okay with that? I wish we had a bed for you."

"It's how I slept at home. I'll be okay."

Opening the thick blanket, Hana laid down on it and covered herself with the other half. As quiet descended upon the hut, she wondered what she'd gotten into. The hut was hugely different than Subira's home, but after Monday, she had no idea what her future accommodations would have been. Maybe they would have been worse than this, or maybe better. In the meantime, she was peaceful and drifted off to sleep.

Chapter 10

Addis Ababa, Ethiopia
Saturday, September 19, 2015

SUBIRA passed a platter of pancakes around the table, followed by a full plate of sliced fruit. The girl's breakfast was subdued as they learned Hana had not been heard from.

Subira said, "I'm guessing Hana won't be returning and I hope she's okay. I can't imagine she ran off, or one of us would have suspected something. Knowing where she came from, I can't imagine she didn't like staying here. In any case, after breakfast, we'll have a day of review about what you've learned in the last ten days.

"As I told you before, on Monday different employers' agents will be arriving to take you to your new job. I know you're ready to go. I've made sure of that. This afternoon, I'll meet with each of you individually to explain where you'll be going and what you'll do. So, finish your breakfast, get your notebooks and Kamali and I will start the reviews."

The girls disappeared upstairs and Kamali asked, "What do you think happened to Hana?"

Subira didn't hesitate, "I don't know where she is, but I'm fairly certain she ran away."

"Why do you think that?"

"It was stupid of me. When we left for Mercato, she had her backpack with her. When I asked her about it, she said she needed it to carry the items she was going to purchase. At the time I thought it was a great idea. Now that she's gone, I suspect she took her things with her."

Then with a surprised look she said, "Why didn't I think of checking her room? Let's go look."

Entering Hana's room, they didn't find any personal items anywhere. Opening the drawers, they found that two pairs of blouses and slacks along with undergarments were missing.

They looked at each other. Kamila said, "She ran off! Why would she do that?"

"I don't know. We've never given any of our girl's a reason to suspect us about anything. Let's keep it to ourselves. We don't want the other girls asking questions. The loss of Hana is going to cost me dearly. Not only in money, but in my personal reputation. I'll lose some respect and trust because of this."

"Hana, wake up."

Hana felt a slight rocking motion as if she was on a boat. She opened her eyes as Amara gently shook her from her sleep.

Rubbing her eyes, she gradually remembered where she was. Standing up, she folded the blanket and placed it in a corner of the small room. Halima was sitting at the table drinking coffee and said, "Come to our elegant kitchen!"

On the table was a plate of sliced bread and a jar of jelly. "Hana, help yourself. Would you like some coffee?"

"Water would be great."

Amara placed a bottle of water in front of her.

Reaching for the bread and jelly, Hana asked, "I suppose you know I have questions?"

"Of course, and we have answers. We'll have some time today to talk through some things with you."

"Amara, why don't you tell Hana your story? I think that'll help her understand us."

Amara joined them at the table with a broad smile. Hana looked at her and was struck by her beauty. But, it would have been difficult to determine which was the more beautiful of the two.

"I'm not sure where to begin. I came to Addis from the far north. The village I lived in was just a stone's throw from Eritrea. It was difficult for my father to find work, so it seemed we were always poor. There were constant skirmishes with the Eritreans since we lived so close to the border, so it was a scary place to live.

"My mother died when I was fourteen and my six brothers, sisters and I missed her very much. We tried desperately to keep our family together while our father searched for work. He spent most of his time cutting wood and selling it at market, which helped but it still wasn't enough. Then, he became desperate. He asked me to move to Addis to work so I could send money back to the family. What could I say? I was sixteen and my younger brothers and sisters were slowly getting weaker. I agreed to go.

"My father found an agent who said he'd take me to Addis and find me a job in a factory. That was four years ago. The man did get me to Addis like he promised, but he forced me to entertain men all along the route. It was horrible and something I try to forget. Then he delivered me to Subira.

"I loved Subira and Kamali and enjoyed the two weeks I spent with them. It felt like they were saving me from a really bad life and preparing me for a good future. That's where I met Halima who's still my best friend. Subira taught us so many things we wouldn't have learned any other way. But the day she sent me to my new job, I went from loving Subira to hating her.

"She sold me to a man who operated a café and disco. The food and music was just a front business for him. It wasn't long until I realized his real business was selling girls for entertainment. It was a horrible life and I finally ran away. But I still blame Subira for what she did. Though she does make legitimate money by providing girls to the factories or families, her real money comes from selling some of the girls to the underground market. The training time is a front. She uses those two weeks to find buyers.

"After I left the disco, I found Halima on the streets and we've stayed together ever since. That's pretty much my story."

Amara looked at Halima and smiled. Halima said, "My story is about the same except for how I got into Subira's program. Everyone in Ethiopia thinks coming to Addis Ababa is the answer to all their financial problems. But, I grew up here and our family was probably just as poor as Amara's. Addis isn't Heaven. Heaven on earth is where you have family and love. Amara will tell you that.

"I remember the two weeks at Subira's like it was yesterday. It was great! Getting to know the other girls was probably the best part of living there, but I did learn a lot. I remember how much I was looking forward to 'The Monday'! We were all excited to know a great job was coming our way and we'd be able to finally send money to our families.

"On my 'Monday', I was sold to a disco, just like Amara. It was a different disco than hers and in a different part of the city. But they were alike. I was forced to entertain the disco's clients and for that I received my room and board but no wages. There was no money to send home and nothing extra for me. If I would've had extra money, I'd have saved it and ran as far away as I could from this place. I suppose that's the reason we weren't paid.

"It's hard to imagine how in one twenty-four hour period someone could go from an extreme high to as low as you could imagine. That's what that 'Monday' was about. That's the reason you're here with us now. We couldn't let that happen to you.

"Amara and I have a life now which belongs to us. We aren't owned by anyone else. Don't get me wrong, our life isn't easy and we're always looking for something better. But for now we're free.

"Hana, I can't begin to tell you how happy we are to have you here, right now, with us. I only wish we could have the other five girls from Subira's with us too."

Amara laughed and said, "Can you imagine how angry Subira would be if we'd been able to get all six girls away from her? That would have hit her right where it hurts! Her pride and her bank account!"

Hana's head was spinning and she was feeling overwhelmed. She said, "Do you have any idea how confused I am? Everything was going great for ten days and I thought the best was yet to come. Now, here I am in a very different place not having any idea where I'm at and what's going to happen next?"

Halima said, "We know what you're feeling. Believe me, when we left the disco we had nowhere to go. We had no job, no money and no place to stay. But, growing up like we did, we knew how to survive. That's what Amara and I've been doing since that 'Monday.'"

"So, where are you working? What kind of jobs did you find?"

Amara said, "Unfortunately, we're doing what we did at the disco. We're entertaining men."

Hana replied, "Why would you do that? It sounds like you're in the same rut you were in at the disco!"

Halima said, "Hana, listen to us. We don't like what we do. There's no way in the world we'd ever choose this life. But, believe me when I say neither of us can go back home."

"Why? Why can't you go back home?"

Amara responded quickly, "Hana, once we were at the disco for even one day, we were branded. Everyone here knows what we do. Our families would be so embarrassed and disrespected in their communities if they knew. We can't go home and do that to them. We'd live in constant fear that somehow, someway they'd find out about our past."

Halima continued, "We're on our own right now. No one owns us! All the money we get, which isn't much, stays in our pockets. We make enough to rent this room and are able to eat. We even have some savings, so we're gradually making headway."

"So how long are you going to keep doing this?"

Amara said, "At the rate we're going, probably another three or four years. Then we'll have enough to start our own business and get out of this work."

"What kind of business would you start?"

"We want to start a business making injera. To do that we'd need to buy an injera cooker and some other things, but we think we'll be able to do that in another three years or so."

Hana hung her head.

Halima looked at her and asked, "What are you thinking, pretty girl?"

As tears flowed down her cheeks, she said, "I haven't done what you're doing, so my family wouldn't be embarrassed. I'd really like to get back home."

Amara softly asked, "Hana, how much money do you have?"

Hana stood up, went to her backpack and retrieved the money she'd received from Kamali to purchase the things at Mercato. Holding it out to Amara, she asked, "Is this enough to get home?"

Amara counted it and gently said, "No, not even close. I'm sorry Hana."

Hana said, "But I can't do what you do. There's no way!"

Halima responded, "You don't have to! But, we do have another idea for you!"

The next morning...

Rubbing the sleep from her eyes, Hana sat up and looked around. It was Sunday, the day before her friends at Subira's would be given their new employment opportunities. For two weeks, Makda, Zoya, Mariam, Lola, Maya and herself had been talking about *'The Monday'*. There had been ten days of training to prepare them for their jobs.

Makda and Zoya had seemed the most excited as each of them had made the decision to seek out a job opportunity. Lola, Maya and she were in Addis because their families needed extra income. They'd made the choice to send their daughters to the capital city.

Mariam, on the other hand was in the toughest spot of all. She'd been kidnapped and treated badly.

Looking around the hut, she thought, how can this be? Here she was, in a tiny shanty at the center of Addis Ababa living with Halima and Amara who were also in a difficult spot in life. The two women had a small income and were participating in a dangerous occupation that was also degrading. Yet, they went out of their way to convince Hana to leave Subira's home and join them.

Hana remembered the difficulty she'd had in trusting them as they tried to convince her of Subira's evil intentions. Their quiet persistence and sincerity had eventually won her over. Only time would tell if the decision to run from Subira had been wise. Right now, looking at the meager hut she was living in, she wondered.

She missed the other five girls and wondered if she'd see them again. Makda was heading to Saudi Arabia so it seemed seeing her again was unlikely.

Halima said, "Hana, good morning. Are you ready for coffee and breakfast? Amara left to buy fresh bread. She'll be here shortly. Come and join me."

Hana got up, folded her blanket and went to the table. She said, "I think I'll have some of that coffee. It smells great."

The door opened and Amara entered. "Good morning Hana. How did you sleep?"

"Good morning. I slept well. Thanks."

As Amara opened the package, Hana caught the odor of fresh baked bread. Soon she had a slice covered with butter and jam. She sipped some of the dark roast highlands coffee and said, "Yesterday afternoon you told me I wouldn't have to do what you're doing. You said you had another idea for me. What are you thinking?"

Halima smiled and said, "You'll find out after breakfast. Seems like your curiosity is rising?"

"Since I left my family in Ropi, nothing seems to be working out like it was supposed to... and yes, I guess I'm curious."

Amara smiled and said, "We understand. Whatever Subira had in mind for you today wasn't going to be a good thing. She's full of promises that are nothing more than empty and evil lies. Your friends are going to have some disappointments today. We were at Subira's too, remember?"

"Yes, I remember."

Amara continued, "We have a job for you. It doesn't pay much but it's respectable work and over time you'll get enough funds to go home. You can go home with your head held high and your family will not have lost respect for how you earned your money."

Halima said, "Let's finish our breakfast and go to Nyala's."

"Nyala? Who's she? What does she do?"

Halima laughed and said, "Slow down, slow down! You'll find out soon enough."

Twenty minutes later, the trio approached a large building. It was two stories tall and had been a factory of some sort years before. The building was constructed of brick but in disrepair. They entered the front door and began climbing a stairway to the second floor.

When Hana entered the second floor, she saw a huge room filled with children, chairs, beds, baby cribs and children's toys. A large woman who appeared to be sixty years old approached them.

"Halima, good morning. It's great to see you. And Amara, it's good to see you too!"

Looking at Hana, she said, "Is this Hana?"

Amara said, "Yes, this is Hana."

The woman pulled Hana to her with a hug and said, "My name is Nyala. It's so good to meet you. Halima told me about you. I could really use you if you'd like to work for me?"

Hana, recovering from the smothering bear hug, said, "I don't know what you do or what you want me to do."

"Oh yes, you're the careful one! Of course. Look around. What do you see?"

Hana paused and said, "It looks like a place for children?"

"Oh my. Yes, it appears that you're also bright!" Laughing as she looked at the many, many children, she asked, "What was your first hint?

"Yes, this is a place for children, but not just any children. Let me explain.

"Here in Addis there are about 140,000 girls and women who work their trade on the streets. Many of the women have one, two or three kids. Some are babies and some much older. But, the problem is they can't do their work when their children are around, so they bring them to me. They pay me to care for them and keep them safe. Addis isn't a safe place for kids on the streets.

"The women work in the evenings and early mornings, so they bring their kids, every day, in the early evening. Then the mamas return for their children before breakfast and take their kids.

"Unfortunately, one of my helpers quit, so I need someone to replace her. If you're not afraid of work, dirty diapers and you love children, I can keep you busy, safe and even pay you for your work. What do you think?"

Looking at Nyala, she asked, "How many kids and workers do you have?"

"That's a great question. Usually we have a hundred to a hundred-fifty babies and kids here. The youngest are about a year old and the oldest are eight or nine. The moms keep their babies with them for about a year so they can feed them between their customers. I have three other helpers, so you'd be busy. I'd love to have you help. What do you think?"

Looking at Amara and Halima she asked, "What do you think?"

Halima said, "You can trust Nyala. Mothers wouldn't bring their kids here if they didn't trust her."

Hana looked at Nyala and said, "Okay. When do I start?"

"If you can come back at six o'clock this evening, you'll work twelve hours. It's a lot of work but it's respectable and necessary. The mothers will adore you for what you do for their kids."

On the way back to their hut, Halima said, "Hana, you can stay with Amara and me if you'd like. You'd need to help out with our food and rent once you get paid, but we'd love to have you live with us. We're really careful about who we open our door to but we both want you to stay. It makes us feel good that we can bring a little bit of goodness into our lives."

Amara added, "We work the same hours as you, so most times we sleep during the day."

Arriving at the hut, Halima unlocked the door and the three went inside. Halima said, "Hana, try to get some sleep. We'll wake you in time to eat dinner with us and get you to work on time."

"I just got up a couple of hours ago, I'm not sure I'll be able to sleep."

Amara laughed and said, "If you can't sleep, I'm guessing you're going to have a really, really long night with those hundred and fifty babies and kids!"

Hana laughed and unfolded her blanket. With the sun shining in through the lone window she shut her eyes.

Late that afternoon, Halima and Amara accompanied Hana to the second floor of the large building and quickly left for their evening work on the streets.

Hana was anxious to see how the first night was going to go and saw Nyala already working with children at the far end of the floor. Her boss smiled as she saw Hana approaching and said, "We're off and running. I'll let someone else take care of these kids and you and I will go meet the rest of the moms when they arrive. They want to know who's caring for their children.

"These women and girls are human beings, but they're treated like garbage. They're used, abused and discarded. But they're some of the most remarkable people I know. They're strong and they're survivors.

"Unfortunately some of the moms are addicted to drugs or alcohol. They think it's the only way for them to get through their miserable lives. Halima and Amara are still young. They're healthy and pretty but their work will take its toll on their health and their looks. Soon, one or both of them will find themselves pregnant. Then there'll be another mouth to feed. We're getting paid to take care of these kids, but the mothers deserve help too. Without our help, the girls wouldn't be able to do what they do. We're a team and my prayer is that somehow things will change so these girls can live their lives in a respectable way God would want for them.

"I know every one of these girls. They're like family to me and there's one thing I know for sure. Not a single one of them chose this life as their vocation. They were either forced into it or lured into it. I know for a fact none wanted it or chose it."

Just then, two girls arrived with their children. Nyala introduced Hana. She looked at the girls and realized that one was likely sixteen years old and the other was probably twenty. They looked tired, but quickly headed back to the street as they left their one-year-olds in Nyala's care. The girls knew if they lingered they'd likely lose a customer. With usually four or five customers a night, the loss of one or two could make the inevitable difference between potential life and death for her or her child.

Hana picked up one of the kids who smiled quickly at her. It was obvious, these kids were very accustomed to being with strangers or caretakers. Hana hugged the little girl and carried her to the far end of the floor where another helper took her. Hana headed back to the stairway where four more mothers were waiting.

One of the mothers brought three children. The oldest appeared to be six years old. Nyala introduced Hana to the mother who quickly smiled and went down the stairs. Nyala said, "She has five children. The other two are older and spend their nights on the street. She can't afford to pay me for five children." Then she continued, "This cycle just goes on and on and on. So, we keep doing what we can to help."

Hana quickly took the three children to a caretaker and returned to the stairs for another three mothers and their kids. Nyala was busy logging in each child in a ledger. Hana could sense the dedication and love she poured into the kids and their moms.

Finally the long night was over and an exhausted Hana arrived home to meet Amara and Halima. Sitting at the table, Halima asked, "So, how was your first night?"

"I'm exhausted! I suppose I'll get used to it, but it never stopped! There were so many kids and only five people taking care of them. I changed so many diapers I lost track. Four of the children threw up and they didn't do it carefully. Usually there was splatter to clean up on three or four others when it happened. I'm not sure how we can keep all of them healthy!"

She rambled on as Halima and Amara listened.

Finally, Hana said, "I suppose this is my new life. I'd like to think I'm making a difference, but this isn't what I had in mind."

Amara said, "Hana, you'll never know what a difference you'll make for these moms. None of us on the streets are making much money. We see others on the streets who simply can't make it. They're slowly starving. There are women out there who can't make enough money to pay Nyala so they try to take care of their kids on their own. But they can't. Then we see the results, as some desperate mothers bring their children into the street business. There are girls out there as young as eight years old doing what we do. Can you imagine?"

Halima added, "... and boys too. It isn't all girls."

"So what will stop this from going on and on?"

Amara said, "If there were more jobs available, that would help. If the factories paid more to their workers, that would help too. I used to think if the government passed more laws prohibiting what we did, that would help. But there are already laws, they're just not enforced. But if they did enforce them, then we'd be without any work and we know what the results of that would be. We're trapped. I don't know the answer."

Halima said, "I think I do. If everyone practiced what Jesus taught, it'd be a new world. The answer is the Bible and what it teaches. If everyone followed what the Bible said, things would be better."

Amara countered, "But, how would that change poverty? We still need food. We need money. We need jobs."

Hana said, "There doesn't seem to be any good answers. But I think you're right about the Bible. My mom and dad taught me about it and I know if we try to get through life without Him, it won't work. It seems like the right thing to share Him with others."

Halima smiled and said, "You might be young, but I think you have some wisdom. Well, time for bed!"

Lying on her blanket, Hana folded her hands and quietly prayed, "Lord, thank you for this home, Halima and Amara, and my new job. I pray for Lola, Maya, Mariam, Makda and Zoya at Subira's and pray they'll get good jobs and you'll keep them safe. I pray You can use me to help the kids you bring to the center every day. I pray I can share Bible stories with them they'll take to their moms. I pray somehow, someway You'll use me for your purpose. In Jesus' name, Amen."

With purpose, Hana closed her eyes and slept.

Chapter 11

Addis Ababa, Ethiopia
Monday, September 21, 2015

MAKDA opened her bedroom door and stepped into the hallway. She descended Subira's elegant staircase for the last time. Her personal belongings and the remaining eighteen small Bibles were neatly tucked in her backpack. She was ready for the next step of her journey which would get her closer to her final stop in Riyadh, Saudi Arabia.

Several of the girls were already downstairs and nervously talking as they awaited their 'opportunity'.

Subira and Kamali had earlier spent time with each of the girls and laid out their individual paths. Of course, Makda was going to Saudi Arabia and Subira had given her an Ethiopian passport.

Subira had said, "You're a special girl, Makda. You have beauty, personality, education and a desire to be successful. It costs a lot of money to get you to Riyadh, but you're exactly what the family there needs. There are thousands of Ethiopian girls finding their way to Saudi Arabia every year, but the Khalil family is looking for someone extraordinary and they're willing to pay the price. You're one of the fortunate ones."

Subira told Lola she'd be going to a wealthy family in Addis as a domestic helper. The family had several children and she'd be helping with the household chores as well as caring for their children. Lola was thrilled as she loved babies and children.

It was obvious to Subira that Maya was a careful and methodical person which made her ideally suited for working in a textile mill. She would be working in a factory which manufactured fabric for the traditional Ethiopian Habeshna kemis and the Somalian guntiino. Both the northern Ethiopian Habeshna women and the Somalian women wore traditional dresses and fabric which suited their cultures. Subira suggested Maya might be able to get a management position considering her cautious, perfectionistic personality and the training she'd just received. It didn't seem to take much education, training or experience to excel above the common laborers in the factories.

Mariam was nine years old and a bit unique. Subira would have her employed in a nanny position with a wealthy family in Dire Dawa, a large city east of Addis Ababa. Subira said the family had one-year-old twin girls and Mariam would be living with a wonderful family.

Subira informed Zoya she'd be working for an Addis modeling agency. Her first assignment would be in a far northwestern Ethiopian city named Gondar.

Makda wondered what Subira would have done with Hana. There was still no indication as to what had become of her and Makda hoped and prayed she was safe. It was difficult to imagine how a thirteen-year-old country girl could survive by herself in Addis.

Makda opened her backpack and retrieved the Bibles. She gave four to each of the girls and said, "I'm going to miss all of you. The time we spent searching for verses in the Bible was special to me. I'm giving you a few more to pass out to others when you think the time is right."

Subira came in from the courtyard and said, "Girls, I have five agents arriving this morning and they'll be taking you to your new jobs. I don't personally have any contact with the places you'll be at. My job has been to make sure you're ready for the work."

The girls sat quietly and waited.

All eyes turned as they heard a knock on the blue steel door at the street.

Watching from the home's front door, they saw the guard open the gate and a short, heavy-set woman entered. She was elderly and simply dressed. Subira looked at Lola and said, "Are you ready? Say good-bye to the others and join me in the courtyard."

Lola stood. Her eyes were moist as she hugged her cousin Maya and then the others. Carrying her backpack, she left the house and met the woman in the courtyard. The girls watched as the steel door to the street opened, closed and then Lola was gone.

The remaining four girls continued talking, making the most of their remaining time together.

The words tumbled out as Mariam said, "I'm scared... I'm not sure I can leave... I don't know anything about where I'm going... You've all been like big sisters to me and I'd like to stay with you, even though I know I can't..."

Then, pausing, she quietly said, "The hardest thing for me to think about is what my family went through when I never came home. I wonder if my little sister Neela missed me as much as I miss her."

"Maya."

The four girls turned to see Subira standing in the doorway. "Maya, your agent is here."

Maya stood and said, "I guess we were so busy talking we didn't even hear the knock."

Hugging each of the girls, she left the room and the girls watched as she was introduced to a young man in a suit and tie. Maya began walking to the gate, then turned and waved at the girls. She disappeared and the steel door clanked shut.

Makda, Zoya and Mariam continued talking until they were again interrupted by a quiet knock on the gate. They immediately grew quiet. A professionally dressed, beautiful young woman entered the courtyard. The girls watched as Subira and Kamali met her. Subira came toward the house and said with a smile, "Zoya, it's time for your future to begin."

Zoya hugged Mariam and Makda and walked to the front door. Then abruptly she turned around, smiled and said, "I'm not sure why I'm telling you this but did I ever tell you my dad called me 'Angel?'"

Then she was in the courtyard, approached the gate and was gone.

Mariam asked, "Why did Zoya tell us about her dad calling her Angel?"

Makda said, "I have absolutely no idea."

Without responding to Makda's thoughts, Mariam abruptly said, "I'm scared."

Makda got up and sat with her on the sofa and said, "Mariam, you've got to be the sweetest person I've known. I've always wanted a little sister and I think God brought me one by bringing you into my life. I wish it were for a lifetime rather than just two weeks."

Then the inevitable knock happened again.

Soon, Subira entered the house, looked at the girls, smiled and said, "Well, Mariam, it's your time."

Nine-year-old Mariam wrapped her arms around Makda's waist for a long time. She followed Subira to the courtyard. Suddenly Mariam gasped. Makda quickly went to the door and saw Mariam cowering beside Subira as they faced a bald man.

Makda heard Subira say, "Mariam, this man will be taking you to the family you'll be working for in Dire Dawa."

Frantic, Mariam exclaimed, "But, Subira, it's Tebeb! He's the same man who kidnapped me and brought me here. You told Makda… "

Subira's slap came quick and hard across the nine-year-old's cheek, accompanied by a sharp response, "Mariam, I want you to straighten up and behave like an adult. I've taught you better than acting like a child. I've known Tebeb for years. He and I have talked about how he treated you and there'll be no more of that. He's sorry for what happened before."

Looking at Tebeb, she demanded, "Tebeb, tell her you're sorry!"

Looking down, Tebeb muttered a whispered, "Sorry."

Subira, looked at Mariam and with a stern voice said, "I need you to go with him… now!"

Baldy reached down and held Mariam's hand. Makda saw terror flood across the nine-year-old's face as the man began walking toward the gate. Mariam looked at Makda with a pleading look and a face full of panic. Then she was gone.

Subira looked toward the front door and saw Makda watching her. Quickly she walked to the front door as Makda retreated into the room and said, "Subira! How could you send Mariam away with that man? I know he kidnapped her and treated her badly on the way here. You told me you would turn him in to the authorities! Subira, she's only nine years old!"

"Makda, I know you're like a big sister to her, but listen to me. When Hana left, it was a huge hit to my profits. I have a lot of expenses preparing you girls for your jobs. There are things I have to do to survive. You don't know what it's like to have a business. The man who just left was sorry for how he'd treated Mariam and promised he'd change if I'd give him another chance. What would this world be like if we didn't learn how to forgive others? Have you ever made mistakes and others needed to forgive you? I know you're a Christian, but wasn't your Jesus all about forgiveness and second chances?"

"Of course He was. But the ones who were forgiven by Jesus gave up evil. Some men tried to convince Him of their sincerity, but it was shallow. They were the Pharisees and Jesus called them 'snakes' and 'fools'. He compared them to cups which were clean on the outside but filthy on the inside."

"Well, I'm giving Tebeb a second chance. Mariam will be okay. Don't worry."

Makda glared at Subira and quietly said, "I guess we'll never know, will we?"

They were interrupted by another knock on the front gate.

Subira walked away as Makda regained her composure. She couldn't believe Subira had slapped Mariam. How could she have done that? What was happening?

"Makda. Come here please." The smile on Subira's face and the sweetness in her voice nauseated her, but obediently she went to the courtyard.

"Makda, I want you to meet Yonas. He'll go with you for the first part of your trip to Riyadh. I've worked with him for several years and I trust him with my best students. The two of you will get along just fine."

Yonas was a young man, probably about thirty years old and was tall, slender and handsome. Makda shook his hand and wondered if his heart was as spotless as his clothing. He was dressed very well and his smile was captivating.

Yonas said, "I'll take good care of her, Subira." Then looking at Makda, he asked, "Are you ready to go?"

Makda wondered what the future would hold. She knew there was nothing for her in Addis and was anxiously, yet with some apprehension, looking forward to her new life in Saudi Arabia. There was one thing she knew for certain... God would take care of her.

"Yes, I'm ready to go."

The two emerged through the blue gate to the street. Yonas opened the door to his newly washed car and she settled into the seat. He closed the door, walked around the car and got in. Starting the car, he merged onto the street. The extravagant house, courtyard and Subira were now part of Makda's past.

PART 3

Leaving Subira's Home

Weeks 4 – 5

September 21 – October 5, 2015

Chapter 12

Addis Ababa, Ethiopia - Monday, September 21, 2015

Mariam

BALDY glared out the side window of the blue taxi as it left Subira's home. The nine-year-old sitting in the back seat with him was softly crying. She absolutely irritated him but he wasn't sure what annoyed him more... her infantile tears or his earlier humiliation when she'd attempted to escape from him at the bus station two weeks earlier. That incident still infuriated him.

One thing was certain, she wouldn't dare attempt another escape. He'd get her to Dire Dawa whether she liked it or not. There was no tolerance from Subira when agents didn't get their jobs done. He was paid only if the 'product' was delivered unharmed and on time. He also knew he never wanted to face Subira's wrath again. She could make life miserable for someone like him. He'd seen both sides of her and feared her like no one else.

Subira had no respect for the agents or for the girls she handled. It frustrated him that everyone had good things to say about her. Though she was heavily involved in trafficking, exploitation and kidnapping, she had an ability to somehow distance herself from anything that seemed illegal or immoral. There were always layers upon layers of people protecting her dirty trade. She had everything to gain and nothing to lose. Schmucks like him were always at the front line taking the hits. He smirked as he thought, 'if only people knew her like I know her'!

The taxi driver stopped at a traffic circle and patiently waited his turn to enter the roundabout. He could take his time as the meter continued running. Baldy glanced at the girl. She was no longer crying, but her face still showed fear. He felt a twinge of guilt, then quickly dismissed it. After all, he had a family of his own to feed and he couldn't let emotions enter into his daily routine. Then Tebeb thought about his own ten-year-old daughter. He hoped nothing like this would ever happen to her. She was precious. Again, he pushed his thoughts aside.

The driver pulled into a parking lot and Baldy paid the driver for the twenty minute ride. He got out, circled around the car and opened Mariam's door. She clutched her backpack and climbed out.

He could see the recognition on her face as they entered the main Addis Ababa bus station. This was where she'd disgraced him two weeks earlier. She'd disappeared and he had to desperately search for her. The temptation to simply let her disappear had been strong, but the potential fury of Subira forced him to continue looking. Fortunately the promise of a few birr coins to multiple vendors brought the desired result as she was found behind a meat vendor's booth. He knew there were some in the bus terminal market who silently laughed at his misfortune and probably hoped the girl would escape, but money, as usual, won the moral debate.

Gripping her backpack, Mariam walked beside Baldy. With her hand tightly clutched in his, she knew there was no chance to escape. Bald Tebeb approached a booth and purchased two tickets for Dire Dawa. The bus agent pointed to a large red and yellow bus in the distance.

Mariam and Baldy walked toward a line of about twenty people waiting to board. The bus's door was still closed and Mariam's hand was still clenched in Baldy's vise-like grip.

The sun beat down on her head as she watched the people in line. A family was laughing among themselves. The children were obviously happy and safe. Behind her a man and woman were talking about a new job he was starting in Dire Dawa. Mariam thought to herself, 'I guess we're both starting new jobs, but I'll bet he isn't being kidnapped'!

She watched the busy station with hundreds of people coming and going. There were vendors everywhere. It seemed everyone was in a hurry. Two women were arguing as they clutched opposite ends of a bolt of brightly colored material. A baby was crying nearby. Mariam saw two men approaching the line and wondered what their life story was. They stopped ten feet behind Mariam and Baldy at the end of the line of passengers. They seemed to be watching her. Then, one of the men walked toward Baldy.

The man asked him, "Where's this bus going?"

"It's going to Dire Dawa."

"Oh, is that where you live?"

"No, I'm from here in Addis."

"You know, I think I've seen you before. Do I know you?"

Irritated, Baldy responded, "No, I've never seen you before."

"No... wait a minute, I'm pretty sure I've seen you before. Right here at the bus station. Why are you going to Dire Dawa?"

Mariam could see Baldy getting angry and he was nearly crushing her hand in his grip.

"Why don't you mind your own business? Where I go is my business!"

The man looked at Mariam and then asked Baldy, "Is this your daughter?"

Baldy now suspected something and said, "No, I'm taking the girl to her aunt's home. She's visiting her for a month."

Suddenly, the second man looked into Mariam's eyes and said, "Is this man taking you to your aunt in Dire Dawa?"

She thought her tiny hand would break. There was no doubt Baldy was sending a message to her via his grip. Who were these men? What did they want? Were they just like Baldy and trying to take her away from him?

Then she thought, 'I don't know these men and I don't know what the motives of these men are, but I do know Baldy's intentions'.

Looking into the man's eyes, she took a chance, "No! This man took me from my family!"

Immediately Baldy dropped her hand and took off at a run. Easily disappearing into the crowd, the two men didn't even try to stop him.

One of the men stooped down and said, "What's your name?"

"My name's Mariam."

The other man said, "Mariam, my name is Nesanet. My friend Yoseph and I have a small organization here at the bus station. We try to find children like you who are being trafficked and exploited. I'm sure you've already been through a lot and you might have a difficult time trusting us."

Pointing to a police officer in the crowd, he said, "I want you to walk over to that policeman and ask him to come back here with you. Okay?"

Relieved, she began walking to the officer. The men saw her talking to him and pointing at them. Then Mariam and the officer walked back to the two men.

Yoseph asked the officer, "Would you tell Mariam who we are and what we do?"

The officer smiled and said, "Mariam, these two men spend their free time here at the bus station helping children like you. You can trust them."

Mariam looked at the three men. Her trust level was low, wondering who was going to take advantage of her next. Was there a chance these three men were working together? Could she trust them?

Yoseph saw the shadow of mistrust in her eyes and said, "Mariam, you're a young girl in a huge city. Believe me when I say we only want to help you. We help a lot of trafficked boys and girls get back to their villages and we'd like to help you."

"I'd really like to go back home, but I don't know where the village is."

"That's what we're really good at. I can hear your accent and I already know which part of the country you're from."

Mariam cautiously said, "Okay... I'll go with you."

The officer smiled and said, "Mariam, you won't be sorry. When you meet Nesanet's wife, you'll be well taken care of."

She noticed, as they walked away, neither of the men held her hand. She knew she could escape if she wanted to. There were enough people around them she knew she could disappear like a rabbit down a hole. But, she continued walking, feeling secure, for now.

Five minutes later, they approached a wooden hut at the edge of the bus station. Nesanet opened the door and she saw a middle-aged woman working at a desk. Mariam was struck by the woman's smile and warm, bright eyes.

Nesanet said, "We need to get back to the buses, so we'll be back later. Adia, this is Mariam."

He continued, "We just found her with a guy who was taking her to a job in Dire Dawa." They left and the woman stood from her desk and asked, "Sweetheart, what's your name?"

"Mariam."

"My name is Adia. Did my husband and my brother Yoseph tell you what we do?"

"Yes." Then she blurted, "I was kidnapped by a man two weeks ago and I'd like to find my family. They have no idea what happened to me."

"Well, we're very good at what we do. We've helped hundreds of children return to their homes and we'll do our best for you too. Okay?"

Aida continued, "Are you hungry or thirsty? Do you need to use the bathroom?"

"Some water would be good."

Aida opened a small refrigerator and gave her a bottle of water. Mariam looked around the small room. There were many photos of children on the walls. Pointing to the photos, Mariam asked, "Who are they?"

"Those are children we've been able to help. We take photos of them when they arrive so we have records."

Looking around, she asked, "Who are the men and women on the wall?"

Aida replied, "Those are the 'known' traffickers. We burn those images into our minds so we can spot them in the bus station. Somewhere in the mix might be a photo of the man who kidnapped you. I'm sure that's how Nesanet and Yoseph noticed you."

Mariam looked at each photo and said, "I don't see him, but I can't believe how many pictures of men and women you have."

"Believe me Mariam, there are many more agents out there we don't have photos of."

Mariam continued looking at the pictures of children. Some were much younger than her and some were older. Her heart broke as she saw the pain in each of their eyes. Some of the children's faces were bruised and bloodied. All of the children looked traumatized.

She asked Aida, "Do I look as afraid as these kids?"

Aida said, "It's apparent to me you've been through some tough things. But you're fortunate because we found you before you went to Dire Dawa. Once you arrived there, it'd be nearly impossible for you to get home. Let's sit down and I'll ask you some questions."

She began, "You said the man kidnapped you two weeks ago?"

"A little longer than that. It took a few days to get to Addis Ababa."

"So, where have you been the last two weeks?"

Mariam was feeling relieved and safe with Aida and her words tumbled out. "The bald man... I called him Baldy... his real name is Tebeb... he took me to Subira. She's a woman who has classes for girls waiting for new jobs. There were six of us there for two weeks of training until one girl disappeared."

Aida was surprised and simply said, "Disappeared?"

"Yes, Hana was with us for about ten days, then two days ago she simply disappeared. We don't know what happened to her. Today she was supposed to get her new job, but I don't know where and what it was."

"Tell me more about Subira. What were her classes?"

"She taught us a lot of things about ourselves. We learned about our strengths and weaknesses and how to react to people different than us. She helped us to speak politely to others as well as how to take care of ourselves. She was paid by employers to prepare girls for their jobs. Subira said she's probably the only one doing this kind of thing which makes her girls more valuable than other country kids."

"Were you comfortable there? Did she treat you well?"

"Oh yeah. It was great. There was plenty of food and we each had our own bedroom."

Aida paused and said, "I've been helping children for a long time but this is the first time I've heard of Subira."

"She said she's been doing it for years."

"Well, I'm not surprised I've not heard of her. People like that distance themselves from the children. They have layers of people bringing the kids to her and layers of people taking them away. Trying to find Subira is like trying to find a tick on a cow. And, believe me, that's exactly what Subira is, a blood-sucking tick!"

Mariam laughed at the thought.

Aida said, "Mariam, it's good to see you laugh. We'll get you home!"

Then she continued, "Well, enough about all of that. Let's see if we can figure out where you're from. Did you come to Addis from the north, south, east or west?"

"I'm sorry. I... I don't know directions so I have no idea."

"That's okay. Can you tell me something about the area where your home was?"

Mariam said, "It was almost always hot and dry. The only trees were along the river. That's where I was when Baldy took me."

"Ah, that helps. That kind of climate could be in the south, southwest or southeast. Definitely not the north. Are you Muslim?"

"Yes."

Aida, looking thoughtful, tapped her pencil on the paper. "When I look at your beautiful dark complexion, I can see you came from the southern part of Ethiopia. But that's still a very large area. We'll need to keep trying to narrow it down."

Mariam was startled as the door to the hut opened. Nesanet and Yoseph walked in with two boys. One was about her age and the other was a few years younger. Their faces were frantic. Mariam thought they looked like small puppies waiting for their next beating.

The boys sat down. Nesanet left and Yoseph began talking quietly to them.

Aida looked at Mariam and continued, "Do you know the name of the river by your home?"

"No."

"What did your dad do?"

"He worked for a man who had a large farm growing vegetables."

"What kind of vegetables?"

"They grew peppers, tomatoes, carrots, maize and sorghum."

Aida, with a smile, said, "This is helping a lot, Mariam."

Grabbing a map, she began studying it intently. Then she said, "Did you live close to a border?"

Mariam's eyes lit up, "Yes! We did."

"Well, there's a lot of desert in southern Ethiopia that joins Kenya and Somalia... "

Mariam interrupted and said, "We lived close to Somalia. My dad told me about the border wars that were fought in our area. He said after the war, the borders changed and many Somalians suddenly found themselves living in Ethiopia. He said we were Somalians in our hearts but Ethiopians by name."

Looking at the map, Aida said, "You gave me two hints. You said you lived next to a river and close to the Somalian border." Then tracing her finger on the map, she said, "There are three rivers that flow from Ethiopia into Somalia. The Gestro joins with the Genale near the Somalian and Kenyan border. They become the Jubba River in Somalia. The third river is much further east and is called the Shebelle. There's a huge amount of desert between those rivers. We're definitely narrowing down your area, but we'll have to do better. Do you remember anything else about the river?"

"No, other than that's where I went two or three times a day to get water for our family. My dad always told me to be careful. The river was deep and sometimes it flowed fast after a rain in the mountains."

"All the rivers in southern Ethiopia have water flowing into them from mountains, so that's not helping."

Mariam was getting frustrated as her hopes of getting home seemed to be disappearing.

Seeing the look on Mariam's tired face, Aida held her hand, smiled and said, "We're not giving up. You hear me? We're not giving up. I want to get you safely home to your family!

"Let's think about this a little more. Did your dad say any more about the river?"

"Like I said, he always told me to be careful. I'm guessing my dad thought I drowned since they knew I went for water. He's probably thinking I ended up in Mogadishu."

Aida said, "What?"

"Mogadishu. He told me if I fell in when the water was high and flowing fast, I'd get a free trip to Mogadishu. He laughed when he told me that, so I think he was joking."

Aida looked at the map and said, "Mariam, look where my finger is. That's Mogadishu, the capital of Somalia!"

Then pointing to a river in Ethiopia, her finger moved, through Ethiopia's southern deserts, over the Somalian border and finally to a city along the Somalian coast. "Look, this is Mogadishu! You lived along the Shebelle River!"

Aida was getting excited and asked, "Which side of the river did you live on?"

Mariam, confused, said, "I don't know."

"Well, when night time came, where did the sun set when you looked toward the river?"

"I had to look across the river to see the sun setting."

"Okay. Okay. That means you lived on the east side of the river."

Looking at the map again, Aida asked, "How did you get to Addis?"

"In Baldy's car at first. Then by bus when we got to the city."

"When you were in the car, where was the river?"

Mariam thought, then said, "We couldn't see it all the time, but there were times I could see it out the window."

"Which window?"

Mariam held up her left hand.

Aida asked, "That means you stayed on the east side of the river. How long were you in the car until you got to the bus?"

"For a little longer than an hour, I think."

"Was the city large?"

"It was huge. My dad told me once, if we'd count all the hairs on our two cows, three goats, donkey and on our family's heads, that'd be as many as the people living in the city. That's where we got on the bus."

Aida smiled. "Mariam, do you see this dot on the map? This is the large city where you got on the bus. It's named Gode."

Aida, held both of Mariam's hands and almost whispering said, "I can get you to your family!"

Mariam screamed. The two boys in the room were startled by the unexpected excitement and watched as Mariam hugged Aida.

Aida put her finger on the map and said, "This is just about where you lived. I'm sure if we drive south a little over an hour from the Gode bus station where you got on the bus and follow the Shebelle River, we'll find your mama and papa!"

Mariam watched as Aida talked to the two boys her husband and brother had brought into the hut. She was asking them questions. The story the boys shared was heart-wrenching. They'd been tending their father's herd of cattle when a van stopped alongside the nearby road. A man brought them bottles of water and began talking to them. It had been as simple as that. Now they were in Addis.

She wondered how many children had entered Addis by buses and hadn't been found. As she looked at the photos on the wall and the two boys, she began to realize just how fortunate she was.

The door opened and Nesanet and Yoseph entered. Aida interrupted her interview with the two boys to say, "Good news! I was able to find where Mariam came from."

Nesanet replied, "That's great. Where?"

"South of Gode."

"That's eighteen hours from here!"

Looking at Mariam, Aida replied, "I'd like to take her myself. I know it's a long way but a bus trip might be a good get-away for me."

Nesanet looked at his wife and said, "I think that's a good idea. You should take her, instead of hiring someone." Looking at his brother, he continued, "Yoseph, what do you think? Can we manage without her for three or four days?"

Looking at the two men, Aida smiled and said, "Yeah right. We know you'll both likely die of starvation without me. You'll probably need to be buried in dirty clothes if I'm not here to take care of you."

The trio laughed as Mariam watched. For the first time in three weeks, her heart was full of joy instead of anxiety and fear. She couldn't believe this was about over. Then the old doubts resurfaced. What if...?

"Aida, there's no way my parents or I can ever repay you for what you're doing for me."

Mariam and Aida had been on the bus to Gode for many hours and still had several hours of travel before reaching Gode.

"Mariam, we don't do this for money. We do this because it's the right thing to do. Our government hasn't paid a lot of attention to what's happening with children in our country. We've heard that maybe next year some legislation and laws will be considered to help stop the trafficking and exploitation, but we need to help kids today. Next year might never come. We don't want girls like you slipping through the cracks."

"So, why do you do this? Were you, Nesanet or Yoseph kidnapped?"

Aida looked at Mariam and said, "No. We were raised in wonderful families and never experienced any of this ourselves."

"Then, why are you doing it? It's costing you money and time."

The bus began braking as a herd of cattle slowly meandered across the roadway. Aida replied, "Yes, it's costing us money and time, but the time is always right to do the right thing." Then looking at Mariam, she asked, "Is your family religious?"

"We're Muslim."

"Doesn't the Quran talk about helping others?"

Mariam remembered a few things from her father's teachings and said, "Yes. My dad said, 'if we remove a misery from a believer, Allah will remove a misery from us on the day of judgment.'"

"See, we both believe it's important to help others who are in trouble."

Mariam reached in her backpack and pulled out the Bible Makda had given her. Thumbing through the pages, she pointed to a verse she'd underlined just a week earlier. "My friend Makda gave me this Book and told us to underline some of its teachings. She said this one is important because it talks about what Jesus did for others."

Aida read aloud from 2 Corinthians chapter 5, verse 21, "'*For He made Him, who knew no sin, to be sin for us...*'"

Mariam said, "Makda told us that God's Son Jesus was perfect and was willing to die for people who were wicked and evil. I can't imagine someone doing that." Then she continued, "Makda also told us we should do the same things for others as we'd want them to do for us."

Then, looking at Adia, she said, "That's what you're doing, isn't it? You put your life on the line for others who can't help themselves?"

"It sounds like you've paid attention to what Makda told you. Yes, the Bible teaches those things, just like you read. I'm a Christian and we try to live our lives the way Jesus lived His. I think you're going to get along in life very well if you live according to what the Bible teaches."

The bus stopped in a small town to give the passengers a restroom break and to get something to eat.

Back on the road, they slept a few hours until they were jolted out of their nap as the bus stopped. Looking out the window they saw they'd arrived at a large bus station.

Emerging with their packs, Aida and Mariam found a bathroom. Then Aida walked toward a food vendor where they purchased injera.

"Aida!"

"What?"

Mariam pointed to a tree and said, "Baldy and I sat under that tree to eat before we left for Addis!"

"Well, let's do it again!"

Mariam was elated. The reality of getting home was becoming more and more real with every passing hour.

As they ate, Aida said, "After we're finished eating, I'll need to find a driver to take us to your village."

Mariam began talking. "I hope Neela's missed me. I wonder who got the water from the river since I've been gone. What are my mom and dad going to say when I see them? Will they think I'm a ghost?" The chattering continued as they walked toward the taxis.

Mariam didn't recognize any landmarks of the passing countryside though at times she could see the Shebelle River out of her right hand window. The air was hot and arid creating its own unique smell and feel. Mariam smiled. She knew they must only be a few miles from her home.

She could barely contain herself. It felt like her heart would soon burst from her chest. She'd never felt an emotion like this before.

Aida said, "This is the only road that follows the Shebelle going south from Gode. Did you live close to the road?"

Mariam tried to recall. She said, "Isn't it strange? I've lived here for nine years and never really paid attention to details like that. Our home was close to the river, but not on this big road. When Baldy kidnapped me, he drove on a dirt road beside the river. We drove on it for about fifteen minutes before we got to this main road."

"We've been on the main road for less than an hour, so maybe we should try to find something closer to the river. We'll turn toward it when we have the first opportunity."

Within a few minutes, they passed a dirt road heading west. Aida had the driver turn around and soon they were heading west toward the river. Mariam could see trees ahead so she knew the river would be nestled like a brown snake between the two banks of trees.

"Look, there's a road!" Mariam was pointing to a dirt road leading south paralleling the river. The driver dodged the ruts and dry potholes as he slowly drove south.

Mariam looked at the sun and knew it was mid-afternoon. Her family would be at home. She wondered what they'd be doing. Then suddenly she said, "There it is!"

Aida looked where Mariam was pointing. Trees?

"That's the spot where I would get our water. That's where I was when Baldy took me."

Looking at Aida, she said, "We can walk to my home from here. Okay?"

Aida had never seen such a radiant smile as the one now on Mariam's face. Her eyes filled with tears as she said, "That sounds good, Mariam."

They got out. Aida told the driver to wait at the river and she'd be back in an hour or so.

Grabbing her backpack, Mariam began walking along the familiar path toward her family's hut. Soon, she could see the thatched roof of their tukul.

Mariam asked, "What if they're not here?"

The hot and arid desert air created a shimmering illusion as she continued walking. Mariam saw someone outside the hut but couldn't make out who it was.

Then she heard a thump, thump as the shimmering heat waves began to subside and she saw her mother beating a rug in the yard.

The beating stopped as her mother saw the two figures approaching. It wasn't often the family received visitors. Shielding her eyes from the sun, her mother kept watching, until suddenly she dropped the rug beater in the sand and screamed.

Two children emerged from the tukul to see what had happened. They saw their mother running up the trail to two visitors. Then, they saw her hugging one of them.

Mariam was crying and laughing and watched as her brother and sister ran to join them.

Finally, Mariam's mother said, "What happened to you? Where have you been? We've been frantic! Your papa has walked for miles and miles downriver trying to find you."

Aida said, "We'll answer all your questions. It might be cooler in the tukul?"

Mariam's mother laughed and said, "Of course, of course. I'm sorry! Please come." Looking at Mariam, she said, "Your father will be home soon from work. I can't imagine what he'll say!"

Approaching the tukul, Mariam stopped at the doorway and inhaled the familiar odors of the fire pit, food and livestock. Then she saw Neela sleeping on her blanket. Kneeling down, she gently picked up the six-month-old and held her. The jostling woke her.

Immediately a smile covered Neela's face as she saw who was holding her. Mariam was crying as she hugged Neela.

Then Mariam heard a noise at the tukul door. She turned to see her dad coming in. He looked at her in disbelief! "Mariam! Mariam! Is it you?"

Neela was almost smothered between them as their father hugged his lost but not forgotten daughter.

Mariam looked at him and realized this was the first time she'd seen him cry. He was unashamed and he hugged her again and again.

Finally, they sat on rugs in a circle as Mariam described the ordeal of the last three weeks. Then, her dad talked about what had happened when she hadn't returned from the river.

"When you didn't return, I went to find you. All I found were your water gourds. I looked along the river bank for some other trace but there was none. Over the next week I walked and walked for miles trying to find you. I asked many people along the river if they'd seen you. No one had. It was like you disappeared into the air.

"Finally, we had to give up the search, but we didn't give up hope that you'd return."

He raised his hands and said, "Thank you Allah!"

Then looking at Aida, Mariam's father said, "Aida, we can't repay you. Our daughter owes you her life as we do." Then quietly and softly he said, "Thank you for bringing our daughter home!"

Aida hung her head as praise was showered on her. She said, "Just seeing your family get your Mariam back is good enough for me. But the real thanks goes to Jesus. He's guided your daughter back home to you. Without Him we would never have started our 'rescue' organization."

Then Aida stood and said, "It's time for me to leave. The driver and car are at the river and I need to catch a bus for Addis tonight."

The family walked with her to the car. Mariam's hands were tightly clasped by both Aida and her mother.

At the car, Aida accepted the hugs of a grateful family and an ecstatic Mariam. Then she said, "Mariam, you've learned a lot these last three weeks and I'll keep praying for you as you learn more about God. You'll have a lot of opportunities to share the miracle of what's happened to you and how God's delivered you. If you read the book of Esther in your Bible, I think you'll see that she and you have a lot in common. I think you'll have an opportunity to help your people, just as Esther did."

Then with another hug and smile, Aida opened the door and got in the back seat of the car.

The family watched as Aida disappeared in a cloud of dust, heading north toward Gode and Addis Ababa.

Mariam's mom and dad each grabbed one of Mariam's hands and the family slowly walked toward their tukul.

Aida looked out the back window of the taxi. Through the swirling dust cloud she could barely see the family reunited with their Mariam.

She turned around and looked out the front window. Now, it was time to get back to Addis and continue her work with more of the last, lost, least and lonely.

She smiled. Her heart was full. She wept.

Chapter 13

Addis Ababa, Ethiopia - Monday, September 21, 2015

Zoya

LEAVING Subira's home, Kadida carefully maneuvered her van onto the busy street. Glancing at Zoya, she said, "Subira told me you were beautiful and photogenic. I see she didn't exaggerate. I think you'll have a great modeling career ahead of you."

Embarrassed, Zoya replied, "Thanks. I was thinking I'd try it for a year and see how it goes. I'm not sure this will be my lifetime career because I hope to be a wife and mother someday."

"I'm sure a year will give you plenty of time to figure out what you want."

Kadida continued, "We'll be picking up three other girls before we go to Gondar for the photo shoot. In the meantime, tell me about your background and family."

Zoya looked at Kadida. In many respects she wanted to look and act as professional as her but that would likely take a few years of practice and experience.

She began her story by describing the life she'd had with her mom and dad in Adama. She shared about the struggle her parents went through to keep her in school which was the reason she was taking the modeling job. She desperately wanted to help her mom and dad financially in their later years. It'd been hard to see them age as they worked harder and longer than most their age.

Kadida said, "I don't see many young people thinking about their parents like you do. Most kids today are very quick to take and not so quick to give. I've always said 'entitlement leads to selfishness'. I admire the qualities and principles you have. Those will serve you well in your new job. Why are you so different?"

"I've never thought about it. I guess I didn't even know I was different. Maybe it's because I'm an only child. I can't rely on siblings to help. It's either going to be me doing something or it doesn't happen."

The van stopped in front of a steel gate. Looking through the decorative steel, Zoya could see a beautiful courtyard and home. Kadida honked the horn and a guard opened the gate. Driving in, Zoya saw eight girls on the porch.

She followed Kadida up the steps where she was introduced. "Girls, this is Zoya. She'll be going to Gondar with Mazaa, Ayana and Afia."

As Kadida went into the home, the girls greeted Zoya with their respectful, welcoming kiss to the cheek.

Zoya asked them, "Are you all part of the modeling agency?"

One of the girls answered, "Yes. Well, at least we soon will be. We just finished a two week course with Madame Gabra. Three of the girls will be going with you to Gondar and the rest of us will stay in Addis for now."

Kadida returned and said, "Ayana, Afia and Mazaa, grab your packs. We need to leave quickly. We have eleven hours of driving ahead of us."

Three of the girls disappeared into the home and quickly returned with their packs.

It was obvious to Zoya as she watched the girls hugging one another that the eight girls had a special bond. It was like the bond she'd had with the five girls at Subira's home.

Zoya sat on a large rock overlooking Lake Tana. The ten hours on the road yesterday and this morning had been tiring. She was glad the driver had stopped for this short rest on the road to Gondar. Below her, a huge flock of lazy white pelicans rested on the craggy and rocky beach. Something unseen startled them and they lifted their heavy bodies into the air and circled the water below.

It was mesmerizing to watch them glide with their eyes on the lake beneath them. Then suddenly one or two would plummet like a falling rock to the surface of the lake, submerging themselves to retrieve a fish.

The girls had stayed overnight in the cool highlands of north central Ethiopia. Zoya was surprised to see how diverse her country was and captivated by the beauty of the passing scenery. The highlands were chilly and she was thankful their van had a heater. She remembered Maya and Lola had come from somewhere in this region. She'd heard them talk about the cool mornings as they tended their family's coffee plants.

There had been a lot of talk among the girls as they made their way to Gondar and Zoya was thankful they had accepted her as a friend.

Each had shared their story of how they'd found a brochure describing the modeling agency. Their individual family situations were all different, but one thing they had in common was excitement for what was ahead.

Zoya was thankful Kadida stopped at this restaurant on the south shore of Lake Tana. They had a catfish lunch that was fabulous. She made a mental note to hopefully stop here on the way back to Addis, if Kadida agreed.

"Girls, it's time to leave. We'll soon be in Gondar."

Piling into the van, they watched as they got a last glimpse of Lake Tana on their drive north.

Ayana looked at Kadida and asked, "Can you tell us more about the photo shoot?"

"Actually, you'll be staying in Gondar tonight. In the morning, a driver will take you to the town of Metemma Yohannes which is on the Sudanese border. That's where you'll have your session. I'm sorry to say that'll be another three hour drive."

The girls groaned.

Kadida said, "Welcome to the world of a professional model. There will be a lot of travel in your future. Usually, you'll need to travel to specific sites because we can't bring the scenery to Addis. This particular photo shoot is for the National Council for Tourism. They're putting together a video and brochure to encourage Sudanese tourists to visit Ethiopia. It's not easy work, but it's a great way for you to see a lot of things you'd not otherwise see."

Zoya tumbled into her bed that night and nestled her head on the pillow. She was tired, but excited. It had been a grueling and long two days getting to Gondar and she wished they'd have a free day tomorrow, but it looked like relaxation was going to be later.

After breakfast, the girls walked to the van and Kadida said, "I'm going back to Addis this morning but I have two men who will take you to Metemma where you'll meet the photography crew. I'll see you in a few days."

Zoya and the girls entered the van and settled in for the three hour drive. She opened her backpack and retrieved her Bible. Opening it, she began reading. She noticed one of the girls watching.

Afia asked, "What are you reading?"

"Oh. This is my Bible." Then she had an idea and said, "When I was in Addis I was with five other girls. One of them gave me a Bible. Before I left, she gave me four more to pass out to others. Do any of you want one?"

Mazaa said, "I'm Muslim. I don't think it's for me."

Afia said, "Me too."

Zoya hesitated and said, "I learned a lot from the three Muslim girls I was with in Addis. They talked about the Quran and we found a lot of things we agreed on. They each took a Bible because they didn't have a copy of the Quran and they thought they could learn some things about how to live from Jesus. Are you sure you don't want one?"

Afia took one of the offered Bibles and said, "I guess it doesn't hurt to learn new things. I've heard a lot of negative stuff about Christians but I've found much of it isn't true. Being with Christian girls has been a good thing for me."

Zoya said, "Growing up in a Christian family, I heard a lot about Muslims. I thought all Muslim's were the same, but now I know that's not true."

Mazaa reached for a Bible and said, "I never thought I'd have a Bible in my hands. Are there any special things in it that would be good for me to read?"

Over the next two hours, Zoya shared her underlined verses with the girls and the resulting discussion was interesting, to say the least.

The van entered a town and the driver said, "This is Metemma. We're right on the border with Sudan and on the other side is a town named Gallabat. I'll take you to the house where you'll stay."

Weaving through several small streets, the van stopped in front of a white wood-framed home. The driver said, "Girls, grab your packs and I'll take you inside."

The girls complied and walked on a concrete sidewalk to the front door. The driver knocked and the door opened. A large burly man opened the door and said, "Welcome. We've been expecting you. Come in!"

The girls filed into the house as the driver got into the van and drove away. Looking around at their temporary home, Zoya thought it looked warm and inviting. She spotted a large comfortable lounge chair and was looking forward to some relaxation.

The burly man led them to a large room at the back of the house. There were several bunk beds by the wall, along with a few chairs. Zoya thought, 'It's not as nice as Subira's, but it'll do'. Throwing her backpack on a bed, she headed for the living room chair she'd spied earlier.

The other girls followed her and settled into a couple of sofas. The man said, "My name is Hakim." He pointed to a heavy-set man in the kitchen and said, "That guy is Kofi." Smiling he continued, "You'll always find him in the kitchen... he likes to eat! We'll be taking care of you while you're here. If you want anything to eat or drink, just help yourself, but you'd better hurry. I think Kofi is just warming up!"

Kofi came into the room and said, "After dinner, we'll take a walk and Hakim and I will show you something really unusual. So, for now, you can relax. Tomorrow will be a big day!"

After an afternoon nap, Zoya returned to the living room and heard sounds from the kitchen. The aroma indicated a great dinner in process. Soon Mazaa, Afia and Ayana joined her.

Zoya looked up as Kofi entered the room carrying four bags. Giving one to each of the girls, he said, "Here's some new clothing and shoes. Like I said earlier, after dinner we're going to take a hike and you may as well get dressed for it."

Mazaa said, "Come on Kofi. Give us a hint about what you're taking us to see."

"I've always known girls are curious, but it's a surprise."

The girls took their bags to the bedroom and changed. The clothing and hiking shoes were all identical. Afia said, "It looks like we're quadruplets!"

Hakim smiled as they sat down in the dining area for dinner. On the table was ample injera, vegetables, bread and fruit. Zoya smiled as she saw desserts on the counter.

Mazaa said, "I think I can get used to this life!"

The meal was just as good as it smelled and looked. The girls began clearing the table when they finished but Kofi said, "You girls are models. Clearing a table isn't part of your job."

Hakim said, "We promised you a hike to see something special. I know it's getting dark, but to see what we're going to see, darkness is a must."

Ayala said, "I can't imagine what we could see in the darkness that wouldn't be better seen in daylight. What is it?"

Hakim laughed and said, "If I told you that, it wouldn't be a surprise, would it?"

Kofi said, "Ready to go?"

Zoya asked, "Should we bring anything along?"

"No. We're fine just like this."

The sun had already disappeared and only the diminishing remnants of the day were still evident. It would soon be dark. There was a half-moon providing some illumination to an otherwise black night.

The girls laughed nervously as they followed Hakim down the street. Fifteen minutes later the last house was behind them and the moon cast an eerie shadow on a dirt trail in an open field.

"I hope there's no bull in this field looking for something to butt!" said Afia.

Hakim laughed and said, "You don't have to worry about that. There's only a few sheep in the area."

Mazaa giggled and replied, "Obviously you've never been butted by a sheep ram! They can do about as much damage as a bull!"

The trail ended at a creek which was bordered by trees on both sides.

"Are you sure you know where you're taking us?" Zoya asked.

Kofi replied, "Of course. We've been here before. Who do you think made this trail?"

Hakim said, "Follow me down the bank. Don't worry, your new shoes are waterproof so you can get 'em wet."

Without hesitation, the girls, one after the other scrambled down the incline, sloshed through the shallow creek and climbed the other bank.

Stopping, Hakim said, "We'll rest here a bit. Make yourselves comfortable."

The girls sat, expectantly waiting for the 'special surprise'.

Startled by the sound of splashing water, the girls peered into the darkness toward the creek. Three men emerged carrying four packs.

Zoya shuddered at the sudden appearance of the men. In spite of the warmth of the still warm air, chills covered her body.

Hakim continued, "Girls, these three men are going to take you the rest of the way. Let me explain what's happening."

With a matter-of-fact voice, he said, "Right now, you're in Sudan. The creek we just crossed is the border and you're here illegally without a passport or a visa. If you were found here, you'd be put in jail where you'd stay for a long time."

Afia quickly understood and said, "No! You can't do this!"

Hakim ignored her outburst and continued, "These three men are Sudanese and they'll be taking you to a van a mile from here. It'll be a twenty hour trip to a city named Abyei. We have jobs for you south of the city near the oil fields.

"I'll answer your next question before you ask it. No, you won't be a model. You've been lied to. Kamali, Kadida, Subira and Gabra didn't have your best interests in mind."

Kofi added, "There's a huge demand for young women in Sudan and South Sudan and we simply fulfill the need. It's called supply and demand. We have to use homes like Madame Subira's and Madame Gabra's to make it happen.

"It takes a home like theirs to find girls for the job openings we know about."

Zoya asked, "Are you saying that Subira and Gabra knew about this?"

Kofi looked at her, smiled and replied, "If Hakim or I had tried to recruit you, would you have come? It takes someone like Subira to convince girls like you. I'm always amazed at her ability to get it done and equally amazed at how many girls willingly get sucked in."

Hakim said, "Kofi and I are heading back to Addis. You'll be in Abyei a day from now. These guys will be driving in shifts all day and night to get you there. We had someone put all of your belongings into your backpacks and had them brought here, so you'll have your personal things.

"Oh, one other thing. Believe me, you don't want to create any issues for these three men. They're some of the most unpleasant men I know and won't stand for any trouble along the way. They understand what I said and aren't disputing the truth of what I've said. Escape? You don't want to do that. Without a passport and visa, you don't exist. You're nothing and you'd be treated worse than a stray dog."

The men brought the packs to the girls while Kofi and Hakim disappeared over the Sudanese embankment into Ethiopia.

All four girls were crying but they didn't utter a word. They followed one of the men down the trail toward a black van.

As the van followed a dirt road through two more grassy fields, they merged onto a paved highway. It was apparent these men weren't novices. What they were doing was standard operating procedure for them. They didn't speak to the girls or to one another. Each had their role to play.

Two hours later, the van slowed down on the highway and pulled onto a small dirt road. There it stopped near a clearing. The van's side door opened and one of the men climbed in. Pulling a leather strap from his pocket, he wrapped it around Zoya's wrists. Pulling it tight, she moaned. The man smiled and secured it to a steel hook welded to the van interior. Then he grabbed Mazaa's hand and pulled her from the van.

Another man entered and pulled a crying Afia out as the third man tugged at Ayala. She tumbled to the ground. He roughly picked her up and carried her away.

Ten minutes later the girls were returned and pushed into the van. One of the men untied Zoya. She rubbed her wrists as the other three girls sobbed. Zoya knew her reprieve would be short.

Back on the highway, the journey into the unknown continued. The next stop, three hours later, gave Zoya her personal glimpse into the evil appetite of her attacker. There was no way to combat the strength the man exerted when he pulled her from the van.

Again, three sobbing girls entered the van.

It was obvious to Zoya that by the time they'd arrive in Abyei, the girls would be broken. There would be no energy left for escape.

A few hours later, the van slowed and the girls cowered together as the van door opened once again.

Zoya, for the first time in her life, now knew the meaning of the word 'hate'. She hated Subira. She hated Kamali. She hated Kadida. She hated Kofi and Hakim. She hated these three men, whatever their names might be.

She knew as never before what 'fear' felt like. When she'd been taken from the van the first time, the fear caused her to vomit. The man had struck her for her involuntary mistake.

The girls tried to talk to the men but were totally ignored as they pleaded again and again for help. When Mazaa was suddenly struck with a brutal backhand the girls stopped pleading. The girls frantically talked among themselves until one of the men slapped Afia. Then the talking stopped. The girls were terrified.

The girls were filled with terror and horror, not only for what they were experiencing, but for what was yet to come.

Finally, after twenty hours, the hell of the trip was over as the van stopped at a small house in Abyei.

Immediately the van's side door slid open and the girls got out. Zoya was amazed that not once in the last twenty hours had any of the men spoken.

Dusk was arriving as the four girls entered the home. They were quickly ushered to a room with four bunkbeds. There were porcelain wash basins by each bed. Zoya looked at her basin and cried as she knew it would take more than a gallon of water and a bar of soap to wash the filth of the last twenty hours from her body.

Full of shame, fear, pain and humiliation she laid on her bed. She wanted to melt into the coarse mattress but knew if she went to sleep she'd still be dirty when she woke. So, she forced herself to get up and wash. Her tears mixed with the cold and soapy water. Then she realized though her body was clean, she'd never again be pure.

Lying down again on the mattress, she prayed as she'd never prayed before. Zoya drifted off to a fitful sleep.

Zoya slowly woke from a night of tossing and turning. Her body was sore, but she was hungry. They'd had very little to eat on the twenty hour road trip to Abyei. She dressed in the clothing she'd worn from Addis to Metemma. The clothing they'd been given for the hike was now dirty and beyond use.

To avoid waking the other girls, Zoya quietly went to the door of their bedroom and turned the doorknob. Nothing. It was locked.

Zoya wondered what the day held on the other side of the door. Returning to her bunk, she pulled her Bible from the backpack. Turning the pages, she searched for a verse Makda had pointed out to her. It was Isaiah 43:2,3 – *'When I am passing through the waters and rivers, God will be with me and the rivers won't flow over me. When I'm walking through fire, I won't be burned and the flame won't harm me.'*

Zoya smiled as she thought of Makda. Then her face twisted into a look of horror as she thought about Subira. Nothing was as it had seemed. If Subira was willing to sell her into slavery in the Sudan, what would Subira do with Makda, Lola, Maya and Mariam? Then she thought about Hana. She wondered what had become of her. Zoya hoped Hana had escaped, but the likelihood of that happening seemed remote.

The other girls began to stir. Sleep had been a welcome companion when fear was all you had while awoke.

A groggy Mazaa whispered, "Good morning Zoya."

She looked at Mazaa and said, "Good morning. I'm not quite sure if it's a 'good morning' or not, but it is what it is. How are you feeling?"

"Probably the same as you and the others. I'm afraid."

Afia responded, "Me too."

Zoya said, "I'm sure we're all feeling the same about that. But, you'll feel better once you're up and dressed. Until we know what's on the other side of that door, it'll be hard to determine what's next."

Ayala raised up on one elbow and said, "My dad was always telling us about African proverbs. We teased him about it, but I think he was wise in remembering them. One he used to say was, *'When a cow is burnt out of his shed, she trembles when she sees a red, fiery sunset in the west'*.

It helps me now to think about him and the old ways. I feel like an old cow that got burned out of its shed. I'm afraid of everything."

The girls laughed, but only for a second or two. Then they remembered where they were and what might be ahead of them.

The bedroom door rattled as the door was unlocked. Zoya trembled in fear. The doorknob turned and surprisingly an older woman stood in the doorway.

With a smile she said, "Girls. It's time for breakfast. Come."

The girls quickly dressed. Emerging from the bedroom they entered a room with a table and six chairs.

Sitting down, the woman and a man they'd not seen before sat at the table with them.

A cook approached with a platter of pancakes and syrup. The girls each took one and poured the hot sticky syrup on it. The couple at the table with them were probably sixty years old and seemed kind.

Finally, the woman spoke. "Girls, I'm going to talk while you eat. I know you don't want to be here, but this is your new home. My name is Izara and you can call me 'Aunt Izzy'. My husband is Zenabu and you can call him 'Uncle Zen'. We're paid to keep you healthy and safe, but you need to know, this home is guarded around the clock. The guards won't let you leave here on your own. There are people who now 'own' you and wouldn't take kindly to having you run off. We've seen it tried, but it's never worked. Those who have tried aren't around to even regret it.

"You've been purchased to do work for the owners. There are several oil fields with a few hundred working men near here. You girls, along with many others, are here for one purpose, which is to entertain those hard working men. All of your room and board is furnished along with your clothing. You'll get a small salary for your work. It's really pretty simple."

Then Zenabu said, "We'll do our best to help you but we aren't able to do you any favors. You don't have a passport or visa and as you know, you're hundreds of miles from Ethiopia. You're illegal immigrants. If you're caught you won't be given asylum here in Sudan and you won't be transported back to Ethiopia. This is your home and you may as well accept it."

Aunt Izzy continued, "Tomorrow's your first work day, so today you'll be free to relax."

Pointing to a door, she said, "Out the back door is a fenced yard. There are chairs there you can use anytime you want."

Pointing to the front door, she said, "Out that door is a guard. Believe me, you don't want to go through that door without me or Uncle Zen."

Calling to the cook in the kitchen, she called for more pancakes.

Zoya briefly stared at the eight foot fence surrounding the yard. Then, tilting her head upward, she saw a large bird circling. Catching a down draft, the bird circled wider and wider, searching for a whiff of dead meat. She wished she had the freedom to come and go like the vulture. She wondered if the bird considered her as carrion, because in some respects she felt she'd already died.

The girls spent part of the day in the yard. Zoya had napped for an hour in the afternoon soaking up the rays of sunshine. They ate lunch and she'd been thankful the food was good.

As she counted the blessings of decent food and the kindness of Aunt Izzy and Uncle Zen, another thought entered her mind. She recalled a story her father had told her when she was about nine or ten years old.

He'd shared an old story about a remote part of Africa. It was a time and place where tribal men fed their captives very well. The prisoners gladly ate the food, but in reality, they were being fattened by their cannibalistic captors.

Zoya wasn't worried she'd be eaten, but in reality, her captors definitely wanted to keep their prisoners healthy. She trembled at the thought, feeling like she was already being picked apart, piece by piece.

"What's the matter Zoya? Are you chilly? I saw you shudder."

Zoya looked at Mazaa and replied, "No. I was just thinking about something not worth mentioning."

The cook opened the door to the yard and said, "It's dinner time."

Gathering around the table, the girls had another good meal. It seemed Aunt Izzy was the talker in the family. She recounted some of her childhood experiences growing up in the Sudanese desert and asked the girls questions about their childhoods.

Though they were in an obviously horrible situation, things could have been worse. Zoya made a mental note to try to think of Bible verses that would help her cope. She remembered a verse in Romans 8:28 – *'We know that in all things God works for the good of those who love Him and are called according to His purpose.'*

How could God be working for my good? The verse specifically said, 'all things'! Was there anything good that could come from this? Why did He bring me to this God-forsaken place? What kind of 'purpose' could possibly be in this? Then she thought, if this place is truly God-forsaken, then maybe that's why I'm here? To tell others about Him? Could it be as simple as that? She made a mental note to ask the girls about it. Right now, she thought the girls would think she was crazy!

Zoya and the girls ate a quiet breakfast. They were subdued. They knew today was their initiation to their new work. Not knowing what to expect, they only knew this would be their new life.

Uncle Zen entered the front door with a man he introduced as Paulos. He said, "Paulos will be your boss. He's in charge of where you go and when. Today, he'll take you to the barracks next to the oil fields. There are rooms for each of you. You'll spend your days and sometimes your evenings there. Men are running the oil pumps and rigs day and night so you'll be needed at various times. Paulos will arrange everything."

Paulos said, "I have six other girls I'm responsible for and you'll meet them this morning when we get to the barracks. I think you know how remote this place is. Without passports and visas, there's nowhere for you to go. Since you're Ethiopian, you don't look like the Sudanese, so you'll stick out like a puppy at a lion party. Unless you think a Sudanese jail is preferable to being in a safe house, you'll obey everything I say.

"Finish your breakfast and we'll be leaving in fifteen minutes."

The girls went to their bedroom, gathered their backpacks and waited in the living room. Paulos ushered them to the van.

The fifteen minute drive to the barracks set the tone for the remoteness of the oil fields. It was very dry and arid. The desert air had an odor of heavy crude oil. They were surrounded by oil rigs, platforms and pumps. There were many round tanks for the storage of the unprocessed crude oil. Paulos explained that the oil would be pumped via pipeline to the Sudanese port on the Red Sea.

Zoya looked at the oil rigs, some of which had flames shooting into the sky from the burn off of natural gas. The desert looked like a wasteland with the derricks resembling antiquated dinosaur skeletons. It was a hopeless place from which there would be no escape.

The van stopped in front of a white building. In the background Zoya could see several large buildings which she assumed were the barracks for the oil field workers.

When she emerged from the van, the heat and the oil smell was almost overpowering. She gasped. Paulos noticed and said, "You'll get used to it."

The girls went inside the white building and realized it was air conditioned! Paulos introduced the girls to a middle-aged woman simply named Madame. She took the girls to their rooms and then brought them back to the main living area.

Six other girls had just arrived so Madame introduced everyone in the group. The girls each gave their names and where they were from. Zoya listened intently but no one was from her city, Adama. But the unusual name of one of the girls seemed familiar.

The six girls all seemed to have a distant and tired appearance. Zoya was thankful to see none of the girls seemed afraid. It looked like time had possibly overcome some of the fear.

Madame said, "None of the workers will arrive for another hour or so. In the meantime you can relax. I'll assign the men to you as they arrive."

Zoya quickly singled out the girl with the familiar yet unusual name and asked again, "What was your name?"

"My name is Eshe."

"Where were you from?"

"I was from Dire Dawa."

With hesitation, Zoya asked, "Do you have a cousin named Behati from Adama?"

With a surprised look Eshe said, "Yes! Do you know her?"

"Behati is one of my best friends. She's the one who… "

Eshe quizzically looked at Zoya and asked, "… the one who… ?"

Zoya responded, "You had asked Behati to join you in Addis. She didn't want to go, so she gave the phone number to me. I went to Subira's but you had just left that morning. We just missed each other. Have you been here for two weeks?"

"Yes, and it's been two long weeks. It's been hard to imagine, but just a month ago I was living with my family and going to school. Somehow, the thought of becoming a model sounded more important than studying."

Zoya hesitated, then asked, "So, what's this life like?"

"The first week was horrible but it's finally starting to be more routine. I don't have any expectations that this life will ever be 'good'. Madame has high standards in the men she allows to come here. That's good for us but it's still a humiliating business.

"These men make very good money but we don't see much of it. Someone is getting very wealthy from us."

The door opened and three men walked in. Madame joined them and took them to three of the girls. They disappeared down the back hallway.

Zoya was apprehensive and her fear was evident in her trembling hands. Soon, the front door opened and four more men walked into the room. Madame brought a young man to Zoya. Without looking at him, she led the way down the hall to her room.

After lunch, Zoya was relaxing with Mazaa, Afia and Ayala. When Eshe joined them, Zoya told them about their mutual friend Behati.

Zoya smiled at Eshe and said, "I can't believe how we could be so far away from Addis and yet be together."

Eshe said, "It's not as big a coincidence as you might think. Subira processes many girls and you and I both responded to the same advertisement about modeling." Then, with visible anger, she said, "I hope someday, someone will shut her house down!"

Mazaa said, "Until the Ethiopian government gets serious about prosecuting people like Subira, it won't end. One of the statistics I read is that over 140,000 girls and women are selling themselves on the streets of Addis. That's not counting the Ethiopian girls who get trafficked to Sudan and countries in the Middle East like Yemen, Kuwait and Saudi Arabia."

Zoya cringed when she heard the words, Saudi Arabia. She wondered what would become of Makda.

Zoya said, "I guess there's not much we can do about any of that from here, is there? But, yesterday I made up my mind I'm not going to sit back and keep quiet while I'm here. I'm a Christian and my Bible tells me this is evil and if these men would think about what's right and wrong, maybe they'd make different choices. They either don't think about it, or maybe no one has ever challenged their thinking. I intend to tell them about my Jesus when I'm with them. I don't have a choice about being with them, but I do have a choice as to whether or not I'm going to be silent."

She continued, "Today my very first customer was young. Right before he left I told him what had just happened was wrong and I didn't want to be here. I told him I was being held against my will. I said Jesus didn't want him here either and asked him to pray about it. He listened to me, but I have no idea if anything will change for him or not. But one thing I do know... I felt a lot better for saying it!"

Just telling the girls about her plan gave her strength. She felt incredibly weak but at the same time, there was an inner strength growing inside her which she knew wouldn't stop.

Then she thought of a Bible verse about weakness and strength. It was 2 Corinthians 12:10 – *'Therefore, I take no pleasure in infirmities, in reproaches, in needs, in persecutions, in distresses for Christ's sake. For when I am weak, then I am strong'*.

Zoya smiled to herself and realized how thankful she was for Makda and those who had encouraged her to memorize scripture.

At that moment, she knew she'd be a survivor!

Chapter 14

Addis Ababa, Ethiopia - Monday, September 21, 2015

Makda

ANGRILY, Makda entered Yona's car. When Subira had slapped Mariam and sent her away with Baldy, a known trafficker of children, she'd been angrier than she'd ever been in her life. How could Subira have done that? Gradually Makda was coming to the realization there was a side of Subira that was dark and hidden.

She'd been so intent on thinking about Mariam's situation she'd paid little attention to her own issues as Subira's home disappeared behind them.

Looking at her guide she asked, "Yonas, Subira never told me her plan to get me to Riyadh. Can you tell me?"

Yonas glanced at Makda and said, "Sure. The bottom line is you're going to get there and there's a family waiting for you to be their helper and nanny. Subira's very good at finding great families for her girls, so there's no need to worry about your job.

"But, there is a glitch. She has great connections and has done this many times, but this time she wasn't able to get you a visa for Saudi Arabia. She was able to get you a passport, but getting you into Saudi Arabia is going to be more difficult without your visa."

Makda felt a sense of dread as she asked, "So, what does that mean?"

Yonas replied, "Well, originally you were going to fly from Addis Ababa to Riyadh, but without the visa, you'd just be turned away when you got there. There's a few factors that make this more complicated. For one, you're only seventeen and that creates different requirements than if you'd be eighteen. Then there's the issue of a tourist visa vs. a business visa. If you were going in as a tourist, you could get that done when you landed in Riyadh, but legally you're going to be there on business. So, we need to be a little more ingenious in how to get you there.

"Since you're not flying to Riyadh, Subira is providing the funds to go by land."

Makda replied, "That will take quite a bit longer, won't it?"

"Yeah, but we'll get you there. Don't worry."

"So, how's it going to happen?"

Yonas replied, "I'm going to drive you to Galafi on Ethiopia's eastern border where you can get a visa to enter Djibouti. Then we'll drive to a village along the Red Sea and Gulf of Aden coast called Obock. That's where you'll get on a boat to cross the Bab al-Mandab Strait between Djibouti and Yemen. Traveling with your Yemen tourist visa, you'll go north across Yemen and cross into Saudi Arabia. You'll be okay, there's thousands of Ethiopians making the trip every year."

"That sounds complicated."

Looking at Makda, Yonas matter-of-factly replied, "We've done it before. We know what we're doing."

She decided to let it rest as they continued their eastward journey toward the Djibouti border. Then she asked, "Yonas, do you have a family?"

Smiling, he replied, "Yes. A wife and two children. A boy who is a year old and a girl who is three."

"Sounds like a nice family. How long have you worked for Subira?"

"I don't work for her. I'm what you'd call an 'independent'. I guide for many people like Subira. It's my responsibility to get people from one point to another."

Makda asked, "Just from Ethiopia to Saudi Arabia?"

Laughing, he said, "No. I also can get people into Sudan, Eritrea, Djibouti, Kenya and Somalia. But usually it's just to another location within Ethiopia."

Makda hesitated, then asked, "How many of those people want to go where you take them?"

Surprised, Yonas looked at her and replied, "I don't kidnap or traffick anyone, if that's what you mean. That's not something I do. All of my customers like Subira know that. I know it's done and it's a sad thing."

He continued, "Just think of me as a travel agent. I help people get to their desired destination."

The next morning, the landscape had turned from green flatlands to rocky desert with scattered hills.

Makda said, "I can't believe how many people are walking along the highway. They're all going east like us and it doesn't seem like anyone is going west."

"Like I told you yesterday, there are thousands of Ethiopians trying to get to Saudi Arabia every year. I'm sure you know the popular myth that if you get to Addis Ababa, you're in Heaven?"

"Yeah, I hear it a lot."

"Well, once they get to Addis and find it's not like they thought, then they buy into the promise of getting to heaven in Saudi Arabia. I haven't been there, so maybe it's like heaven. Who knows? From what I hear about the Khalil family, I think you'll be happy."

At noon they came upon a long line of trucks. Yonas said, "This is the border checkpoint for Galafi, Djibouti. It'll take us an hour to get through the border checkpoint. When we get to the guards, give them your passport and tell them you want a tourist visa. I'll pay for it and we'll be on our way."

Makda asked, "We saw so many Ethiopians a few miles back walking toward the border, but I don't see any here. Why?"

Yonas replied, "The refugees meet smugglers in the desert near here and pay them to lead them down the trails and into Djibouti. That way they miss the checkpoint. When we're on the other side we'll start seeing them again. In fact, you won't believe how many there'll be. Sometimes it's like watching a trail of ants. You don't know where they're coming from, but you do know where they're going."

"Where are they going?"

"To the same place you're going. Obock. It's where the boats are."

Makda asked, "Why do you call them refugees? I thought a refugee was someone who had to leave their country because of persecution or war?"

"I'm sure that's true, but these Ethiopians are the poorest of the poor. They aren't escaping war. They're trying to survive by escaping poverty. Unfortunately for them, it's going to get much worse."

"Why do you say it'll get worse for them?"

Yonas explained, "They save their money for months, even years. Then when they can't take their situation any longer, they start walking. They don't waste their money on a car ride. We've driven twelve hours to get to this spot and I'm sure you now realize how fortunate you are. Most of these people have walked that five-hundred miles and it's taken them maybe a month to get here. They'll pay the border smuggler to get them across. The rest of their money goes for the boat ride.

"Usually most run out of money when they reach Yemen. With thousands and thousands of refugees there, they can't find a job. So, again, they start walking north toward Saudi Arabia. Sadly, the best part of the trip for these people is here in Ethiopia. Yemen is a hell-hole for them."

Makda said, "I had no idea."

Yonas replied, "Most people don't. But it's a scene that plays itself out every day, every week, every month and it's been happening for years."

"So, what happens to me when I get to Yemen?"

Yonas smiled and said, "Fortunately you have a great travel agent! I have a driver named Haji lined up for you on the other side. I've never met him but he'll be your 'Yemeni Yonas'. I've used him many times and he's very good at what he does. You'll be okay as long as you listen to him."

Makda noticed there was only one truck separating them from the border guards so she retrieved her passport. The truck began blowing thick black smoke from his exhaust as it slowly moved forward.

A tired guard in a khaki uniform approached the car. Yonas and Makda handed him their passports. Makda said, "I need a tourist visa."

Yonas handed some currency to the guard who disappeared into an office as two armed men watched their vehicle.

Soon he came back with the passports and visa and waved them across the border.

An hour later Yonas said, "We'll be at the coastal village of Obock in about three hours. In the morning you'll get on your boat."

Makda said, "Now I know what you mean about seeing more people again. We must've passed twenty-five or so walking just this last mile."

"Yeah, it'll be like that for a while."

Then Makda said, "Look! There's a mother with a baby sitting beside the road. Let's give her a ride."

Quickly, Yonas replied, "No. We can't. If we're caught giving these illegals a ride I could get arrested for trafficking and smuggling. I can't let that happen."

"If they're illegal, why doesn't the government arrest them?"

"And do what with them? They can't keep 'em out of their country so they're just happy to let 'em pass through as long as they don't stay. The path is clear to Obock."

"So, why would they arrest you?"

Laughing, Yonas said, "Economics. I have money and a car! They know they could get something from me, but they can't get anything from the illegals."

Pointing ahead, he said, "Do you see that rocky ridge up ahead?"

"Yes, why?"

"We'll stop at the top and I'll show you something."

A couple of miles later, Yonas parked the car alongside the road and got out, motioning Makda to join him.

She couldn't believe how hot it was. It was sweltering and made her realize she'd taken the car's air conditioning for granted.

Leaving the roadway, they walked a hundred feet to the top of a ridge. Yonas pointed to the desert and asked, "Do you see the line of people walking? They'll be at the boat docks tomorrow, if they make it."

"What do you mean, if they make it?"

"Many die along the way. Others on the trail cover them with sand or rocks and continue on. There are hundreds, maybe thousands of corpses lying here in the desert. All of them had hopes for a bright future in Saudi Arabia.

"A month ago I heard about an Ethiopian who had made his way all the way to the Saudi border only to get caught. He was imprisoned for six months before making the return trip. He told me those who died in the Djibouti desert were the fortunate ones. Those who made it into Yemen had to endure much more."

Walking back to the car, Makda's heart broke for the poor in Ethiopia. She'd had no idea. It was like God had just pulled the covering off of a real-life hell she never knew existed.

After an hour of driving, the Gulf of Aden appeared out her right window. It was a magnificent view and contrasted heavily with what she'd been learning about the ugliness of poverty and hopelessness.

Then Yonas said, "Just ahead is Obock. I'm not sure what you've envisioned about your boat ride, but maybe I should give you a hint. The boats are wooden fishing boats. They're designed to hold a hundred people but they crowd about one-hundred and fifty into them for the trip. I wish I had something better for you, but that's the best there is. On the other side my friend Haji will find you. His air conditioned car will get you to the Saudi Arabian border."

He parked the car alongside the road. Makda saw several hundred people on the beach. Some were crowded under tarps but most were being slowly roasted by a blazing sun. The beauty of the Gulf was likely not even noticed by those seeking to survive yet another day.

"Yonas, would it be okay to walk on the beach?"

"Are you sure you want to do that?"

Hesitating, Makda said, "Yes."

Yonas locked the car and they began walking among the people. There were groups of two, ten or twenty spread sporadically across the beach. Walking slowly, Makda saw many young men in their teens or twenties. There were a number of single young women but very few older people.

The people had been walking for days over rocky, rough and hot terrain. She saw many with blistered and bleeding feet. A young girl with blisters on her face held out her hand to Makda. The hot desert sun had taken its toll in several ways.

A boy about ten years old rubbed his stomach with one hand and held out his other for food. She had nothing to give.

In another group, a mother was silently weeping as she looked at the still and quiet body of her two-year-old daughter lying in her lap.

Makda looked at Yonas and said, "I think I'd like to go back to the car now."

Returning to the car, Yonas opened the trunk and retrieved two bottles of water and sandwiches. It was difficult for Makda to eat as she thought about the wretched poverty and suffering only yards away.

After eating, Yonas said, "The first boats will be leaving at dawn. I'll get you on the first boat so it'll be good for you to get some rest now. Over the next couple of days rest won't come easy when you're in Yemen. You're going to see and learn a lot and those'll be things you wish you hadn't seen or experienced."

At dawn Makda opened her eyes. She heard people talking outside the car. She noticed Yonas was awoke and she asked, "Is it time?"

"Yeah. It's time. Grab your bag and let's head over to the boats."

Making sure she had everything, Makda followed Yonas over the sand to the shoreline. She saw a large, wooden fishing boat about thirty feet long bobbing up and down with the waves. There was a crowd of people congregating around a man standing at the water's edge. Yonas approached him and began talking, though both were being jostled by the group. He handed something to the man and then pointed at Makda. The man motioned for her to come.

Yonas said, "Makda, I've paid him so you'll be one of the first ones to get on the boat. Hold your place, okay?"

He continued, "When you get to the other side my friend Haji will be waiting for you. He'll have on a yellow baseball cap. He'll get you to Saudi Arabia. It's time to go. Safe travels."

Makda gave him a quick hug, uttered a thank you, and approached the man. He pointed to a spot and said, "Stand right here until I have a group of ten people, then start walking through the water to the boat when I tell you. Someone will help you get in."

Standing ankle deep in the Gulf of Aden, she looked at the boat and then the crowd of people trying to pay. She smiled to herself and thought, 'if only my friends could see me now!'

Then the man shouted at her and said, "Go! Start walking. Hold your backpack over your head."

Makda began walking. Fortunately the water was relatively calm and she continued moving toward the bobbing boat. Another fifty feet. How deep would it get? Already it was up to her waist. Another twenty feet and it was up to her chest. Then she was there, alongside the rough wooden hull.

Two strong arms reached down and pulled her over the bulwark and into the boat. Drenched and stumbling, she quickly moved to the center of the empty boat and sat on a rough wooden seat. She watched as more men and women clambered aboard.

Shivering, she sat in the breeze with her wet blouse and slacks. She looked back toward shore and saw another group of ten people in the water and another group waiting on shore. She was amazed at the efficiency and speed with which the boat was being filled. Then she remembered this wasn't the boat's first trip. Yonas had said these boat trips went on day after day. It was difficult to imagine there were so many desperate people from her beloved country searching for hope elsewhere. How could that be? Then, suddenly, she realized she was no different than the other one-hundred and fifty bedraggled souls surrounding her. They were all searching for a better life in a better place where they were no longer helpless and hopeless. She admired the tenacity and strength of her wet companions.

Soon, the full boat, lurched forward as the motor coughed to life. There were men and women standing alongside the bulwark trying to maintain their footing.

Makda looked at a young girl sitting beside her, smiled and said, "My name is Makda, what's yours?"

Shyly the girl said, "Kayla."

"How old are you?"

"Fourteen. How about you?"

"I'm seventeen. Are you alone?"

Kayla replied, "Yes. My parents died and I didn't have anyone to live with, so I was living on the streets in Addis until I decided to join a group going to Saudi Arabia."

Makda said, "My parents died in a car accident, so I know what it's like being alone."

The three-hour, sixty-mile boat trip across the Gulf of Aden went quickly as Kayla and Makda talked. Makda desperately wanted to ask

Kayla to come with her in Haji's car to Saudi Arabia. But, Kayla was an illegal and her presence would likely jeopardize Haji, so she decided to wait until she could ask him.

Excitement stirred among the passengers as they drew closer to the Yemeni shoreline. Makda stood to see what was ahead. She saw a beach with a few fishing boats and ten or so men waiting.

The boat stopped about fifty feet from shore and anchored. The motor stopped and all was quiet except for the lapping of ripples against the hull. A few of the men from shore waded into the water to help the passengers get over the bulwark. Suddenly, too many of the passengers began moving toward the shore side of the boat and it began tipping. Two of the men began yelling and hitting some of the passengers to force them back.

Then, the travelers methodically began climbing overboard with the help of the men in the water. Makda and Kayla climbed over the rough wooden bulwark, holding their packs high above them. With their feet on solid ground once again, they began the short walk to the shore line.

Makda, dripping wet from her walk ashore, looked around. She saw Kayla sitting on the sand and her heart broke. Fourteen years old, alone, parentless, hopeful for a future, yet helpless. Walking up the short incline of the beach she reached the top and saw a desolate desert landscape. Her fellow passengers were walking north in their persistent search of hope and fortune in Saudi Arabia. There were four vehicles off to her right so she began walking toward them. Then she heard someone yell, "Makda!"

Turning around a young man with a yellow baseball cap walked toward her and said, "Are you Makda?"

"Yes."

"Great! I'm Haji, Yona's friend."

Makda breathed a sigh of relief and said, "I'm really glad to see you. I wasn't looking forward to a long walk!"

"You're right. It is a long walk! A three-hundred mile walk, in fact. And that's just to the Saudi border."

Makda said, "I can't imagine. These people have already walked halfway across Ethiopia and still have this ahead of them."

"Let's get to the car, okay?"

Makda said, "Haji, I was wondering if you'd be willing to take another passenger? There's a fourteen-year-old girl I met on the boat who's all alone. I could pay you something for the trouble."

Haji replied with a smile, "Well, let's go meet her. I have to be really careful who I give rides to. You have a passport and I'm guessing she doesn't. If I'm caught transporting illegals, there's a price to pay. Either I go to jail and probably lose my car, or I pay a bribe to whoever caught me. But, let's go talk to her."

Makda pointed to Kayla who was still sitting on the beach. No doubt, she was overwhelmed and had no idea what to do next.

"What's her name?"

"Kayla."

Haji called to her, "Hey Kayla."

Kayla turned and saw Makda and a young man. She stood and began walking toward them.

"Hi Kayla, my name is Haji. Where are you going?"

"I want to go to Saudi Arabia and find work."

Haji asked, "Do you have a passport and visa?"

With downcast eyes, Kayla responded, "No."

Haji looked at Makda and then back to Kayla, "I'd be taking a huge chance if I took you with us." Then he said, "Tell you what. I'll at least take you to the border if you want to travel with us?"

Kayla's face beamed as she said, "Yes! Thank you so much!"

"Well, let's go", he said, leading the way to his car.

As he opened the front door for Makda he said, "You should have some documents from Yonas for me?"

"Oh yeah. Reaching in her backpack she pulled out an envelope."

Haji opened it, began reading and finally said, "This is what I needed. Your passport and the verification letter from a woman named Subira that you actually have a job in Riyadh with a Khalil family."

Pocketing the envelope, he said, "Let's get on the road."

They drove for twenty minutes until Haji turned off the road and parked beside a few other vehicles. Makda noticed a building alongside the road.

"Wait here, I need to talk to someone. I'll be quick."

The girls got out of the car as Kayla said, "Makda, thanks for taking me with you."

"Don't worry, I'm happy to be able to do it. I wouldn't have wanted to see you make the three-hundred mile walk to Saudi Arabia."

Haji came out the front door with two men. One of the men was holding her envelope and immediately Makda felt fear. Approaching the car, Haji said, "You'll need to go with these guys for a few days, but don't worry, they're friends of mine. Just do as they say and you'll be fine."

Makda said, "Haji, what's going on?"

One of the men said, "Girls, come with me."

"Haji, don't do this! What's happening?"

"Just do as they ask and you'll be okay. I'll be back to pick you up in a few days."

One of the men grabbed Makda's wrist and pulled her toward the front door. She turned and saw the other man firmly grasping Kayla's arm. Then she saw Haji getting into his car.

They walked through the front door and down a dimly lit hallway. The man leading her opened a door and pushed Makda inside. The second man did the same with Kayla.

Makda stumbled and fell. The sunlight streaming in from a window revealed two other girls and a guard. Thoroughly frightened,

Makda pulled a whimpering Kayla toward her as they sat in a dim corner.

The two men left and Makda asked one of the other girls, "What are we doing here?"

"We don't know. We came on a boat from Ethiopia yesterday and were brought here. They haven't told us anything."

The guard said to the four girls, "You'll be leaving here soon enough." Then with a grin and pointing at Makda, he continued, "We were waiting for you. I didn't know you'd be bringing your little sister with you."

Makda replied, "How could you know I was coming? Who told you about me?"

The guard smiled and said, "We knew about you before you ever left Addis. There's many slices of bread between Addis and Riyadh. Each of them need their slab of butter!"

Makda trembled as she felt a premonition of the unknown. Looking at Kayla, she held her tighter as if the warm embrace would protect her from what was to come.

A man entered the room and said, "It's time to go. Grab your belongings and come with me."

The girls stood and followed him to a van parked next to the building. Pushing them inside, he and another guard got into the front seat.

The van headed east following a meandering and dusty desert road. Fifteen minutes later they drove up to a hut. The walls were mud daubed and the tin roof was rusty. The front door was steel with a heavy padlock.

Pushed into the hut, they saw three girls sitting on mats on the wooden floor. The door behind Makda clanked shut with a thud and they heard the lock click.

Makda looked at the three girls. They weren't smiling.

She asked, "What's this place?"

A girl who looked to be about twenty years old said, "We have no idea."

"How long have you been here?"

"About a week."

Makda recoiled as she asked, "Why are you here?"

One of the other girls who was probably sixteen said, "Who knows. When we arrived here on a boat, we began walking north toward Saudi Arabia. A van stopped us and demanded to see our passports. We didn't have any, so they arrested us and brought us here. They've treated us okay, but it seems like they're waiting on something to happen. I don't think it'll be anything good."

The door opened and a guard pointed a thick, stubby finger at Makda and said, "Come with me."

Makda stood with a brave face and followed him.

Entering another room, she saw a man at a desk with a computer and several other pieces of electronic equipment. The guard pointed to an empty chair in front of the solitary desk. She sat down.

The man at the desk said, "Makda. It's good to finally meet you. I've heard a lot about you."

"How have you heard about me?"

He held up the envelope and said, "I've known about you for probably three weeks, even before I was handed this envelope!"

"How could you have known about me before today?" Then suddenly she remembered there had been another side of Subira which had been well hidden. What had happened to Mariam was likely happening to her. She didn't need any answers from this man.

Glaring at the man, she asked, "What's your name?"

Smugly, he smiled and said, "I don't have a name, Makda. If you need a name, use 'Sir'."

He was middle-aged and rough. Though his clothing was clean and neat, he'd obviously lived a harsh life.

Holding her envelope in his hand he opened it and laid the papers on his desk. Reading quietly to himself he finally said, "I see your parents died in a car accident and you're on your way to the Khalil family in Riyadh. It says you have no family other than an uncle named Gyasi."

Makda said nothing.

Continuing, the man said, "You provided Gyasi's contact information when you filled out your application several weeks ago. I think I need to contact him and let him know you're in a dangerous situation. Will you give me permission to get in touch with him?"

Emphatically, Makda said, "No!"

Smiling the man said, "That's fine Makda. Then you're of no use to me. I'll have to find another way to get value out of you."

Hesitating, and less confident, Makda asked, "Why do you want to contact my uncle?"

"I'm guessing since he's family, he'd want to make sure you stay safe. That's what family is all about, right?"

Again, Makda was silent.

"Tell you what, I'll give him a call and see how much you mean to him. I don't need your permission for that."

He stood up from his chair and Makda noticed how thin he was. She made a mental note to call him 'Stickman'. She smiled to herself as she recalled Mariam giving the name of 'Baldy' to her abductor.

A guard took her back to the other girls.

Kayla asked, "What happened?"

Makda explained and Kayla said, "I don't have anyone back in Ethiopia for him to call."

Two hours later, the guard took Makda back to the office. Stickman said, "I was able to talk to your uncle. I explained your situation to him and he got angry. He told me he's an attorney and there's no way he'll help by giving me money. I told him if he cares about you, he'll send us $50,000! I gave him my number and told him to call me back in five minutes. He did."

"What did he say?"

"He said he can't get me that kind of money, so I hung up."

Makda asked, "You're asking him for money? That's kidnapping for ransom!"

Stickman smiled and said, "Yeah, that's right. Kidnapping for ransom. Are you an attorney like your uncle? Those are pretty big words for a young girl."

Makda replied, "I can't imagine how much trouble you'll be in when you're caught."

With a self-assured grin, he replied, "I've been doing this for more years than you can imagine and haven't been caught yet. Because I'm so experienced at this, I know your uncle will be calling back sometime in the next couple of days and offer me $1,000. I won't say 'yes' or 'no', I'll just hang up again. This'll go on for a few days, so you may as well get comfortable with your friends."

Back in the room, Makda told Kayla and the girls what was happening. One of the girls said, "It seems you're the only one with family that can help. Our families don't have anything to give. We're stuck."

Another girl said, "Letting us go would be like throwing money into the wind. They want to get something from us, but we don't have anything to give."

Makda looked down and knew that wasn't the case. She looked at Kayla and her heart broke.

That evening, a guard entered the room and took two of the girls with him. Thirty minutes later they returned. One of the girls had a large bruise on her face.

The two girls sat on their mats with their knees drawn tightly to their chest and cried.

The next morning Kayla was taken from the room. There was a quick and fearful glance back to Makda as the fourteen-year-old went through the door. Moments later the girls heard Kayla scream as a car door closed. Then a car's engine started and Kayla was gone.

It had been four days since the boat ride across the Gulf of Eden and Kayla hadn't returned. Makda was devastated. If only she'd not given Kayla a ride with Haji she'd probably be safely on her way to the border.

The door to the girl's room opened and a guard motioned for Makda to follow him. Entering the office, she sat in the chair in front of the desk.

Stickman arrived and sat down. "Makda, I've heard back from your uncle two times. It seems like we're stuck. He offered me $1,000 which of course I refused. Then he called back this morning and offered $2,500. He's a stubborn man."

Immediately Makda said, "Where's Kayla?"

"Who?"

Angrily, she spat the next words, "The fourteen-year-old girl you took yesterday from our room. She has a name! Kayla! What did you do with her?"

"Oh. Her? She got what she wanted. She has steady work. That's what she came her for."

Subdued, Makda asked, "What's she doing."

Stickman simply leered at her and said nothing.

"What's she doing?"

"Well, there's probably only a few things she can do. She came here with no experience and without money." Shrugging his shoulders, he asked, "What could she do?"

Though Makda was hoping her own situation would improve, her future plans were rapidly dimming. She asked, "So, what are you going to do with me if my uncle pays?"

Stickman leaned forward and said, "It appears you're protected. The Khalil family in Saudi Arabia is very important and have a long reach. It seems it even reaches to us 'poor folks' in Yemen. When your Uncle Gyasi pays, Haji will take you to the border and all will be well. Consider this stop-over with me as a minor detour and inconvenience."

"My uncle won't pay."

"Of course he will. It's just a matter of when."

The next morning, the door opened and three more unkempt, young girls entered. They huddled together on a mat in one of the corners. A guard then motioned for Makda's earlier roommates to follow him.

Once again, Makda heard car doors close and a car leaving. Did this cycle of misery ever stop?

She looked at the three girls. All were probably teen-agers from Ethiopia. Then their questions spilled out as they sought to make sense of where they were and what would happen next.

She was frustrated she couldn't give them any hope. She knew what their future was and certainly didn't want to share her own. Makda knew she was among the fortunate. She had a passport, a job opportunity with a wealthy family and an uncle with money. She felt ashamed.

The next morning, the door opened once again and Makda was told to follow the guard. Stickman was waiting for her in his office and said, "Good news. Uncle Gyasi's finally come through for you. It seems that he does love you. You'll be able to leave with Haji."

She couldn't imagine what her uncle's family had gone through in finding the funds to fix her problem.

Reaching behind his desk he grabbed her backpack and threw it to her. It landed on the floor with a thud. Picking it up, she wondered if everything was still intact. Then she listened as Stickman droned on and on about how sad he was in how she'd been treated. He told her to say good things to the Khalil family about how she'd been treated in Yemen. As he talked she saw one of her Bibles on his desk.

Finally, when Stickman was done talking she said, "I see one of my Bibles must've fallen from my pack onto your desk?"

Glancing at it he said, "Oh, is that yours? Yes, it must've fallen out. Do you want it back?"

Smiling, Makda remembered her pastor's words four weeks earlier when he'd given her the twenty-four small Bibles. He'd said, *'Here's more food for hungry souls. It's guaranteed if you add the 'salt of the earth' and the 'light of the world', God will bless those efforts and bring a harvest.'*

Makda looked at Stickman and said, "No, you can keep it. In fact, I've underlined some important things in it for you to read." Then knowing she was pushing her luck, she said, "If I let you keep the book, will you promise to read what I underlined?"

"Of course. I'm an educated man and always willing to learn more about life."

Then he said, "Haji's waiting for you outside. It's time to go."

He stood and seemed to be expecting something from her. A handshake? A thank you? A hug?

Makda turned and walked out into the brilliant sunshine. Haji was standing by his car and opened the door for her. Makda wondered what had become of the three girls who had left yesterday. She wondered what would happen to the three who had just replaced them. She wondered about the hundreds who would be passing through this hell-hole. She shuddered as she entered the car. She didn't even look at Haji.

Haji seemed genuinely ashamed as he tried multiple times to start a conversation with Makda. Instead, she continued to look at the desolate landscape out her window. She was amazed at the hundreds of people they'd passed in the last four hours. The three-hundred miles to the Saudi border were swallowed quickly as Haji seemed anxious to rid himself of this guilt-producing girl.

Finally Makda asked, "Haji, how can you be a part of all this?"

Glancing at her, he replied, "What are you talking about?"

Glaring at him she said, "The trafficking, kidnapping, exploitation, abuse, prostitution! You're just as guilty as Stickman?"

"Stickman? Who are you talking about?"

Makda didn't answer and looked out the window at a struggling woman with two small children walking beside the road.

Finally, Haji said, "I have to make a living too. I'm not responsible for what happens to people. I'm just a driver. I have to follow the rules of the locals. If I don't, my family and I will pay a price."

Angrily she said, "Haji, God says in James 4:17, if any person knows of a good thing they should do and they don't do it, it's sin."

He snapped back, "Just be happy I'm taking you to the border. I'll really be happy when you shut your mouth!"

Makda smiled as she silently thanked God for a pastor who had encouraged Bible memorization. She said to Haji, "God says in Matthew 18:8-9 – *'If your hand or foot causes you to sin, cut it off and cast it from you. It is better for you to enter into life lame or maimed, rather than having two hands or two feet, to be cast into the everlasting fire. And if your eye causes you to sin, pluck it out and cast it from you. It is better for you to enter into life with one eye, rather than having two eyes, to be cast into hell fire.'*"

Then she continued, "God also said in Matthew 22:39 that we should love our neighbors just like we love ourselves. In Luke 6:31, it says we should treat others the same way we want to be treated."

She looked at Haji who was quietly watching the road in front of him. Makda looked ahead and saw a woman sitting on the side of the road and quickly said, "Haji, stop the car."

Fearful of another scolding, he complied.

She got out of the car and began walking toward the woman. Haji yelled at her and said, "Makda, don't do this! Get back in the car!"

She continued walking and knelt beside the woman.

The woman was leaning forward and not moving. Makda shook her and finally the woman tilted her head up. Her eyes were matted and barely open. Haji stood over both of the women and said, "Makda, get back in the car. Now!"

Makda stood and looked at Haji and said, "God said in Proverbs 28:27 – *'Those who give to the poor will lack nothing, but those who close their eyes to them receive many curses.'* Look at this woman Haji! She has nothing. If you walk away from her you're going to receive curses in your life! If you help her, God will bless you. How could you walk away from this poor woman?"

Haji looked at Makda, then at the woman. Then he turned and looked down the road. "Makda, you're a real pain... a nagging, never-ending pain! There's no end to the people needing help. Once you start, where do you finish? If you give help to one, what then?"

Makda felt a twinge of compassion for him as she said, "You're right, I don't know where to stop. But in front of you right now is one woman who needs help. If we leave her, she'll probably be dead in an hour. What are you going to do?"

Haji was obviously compromised and frustrated. He felt like he'd just been check-mated in a chess game. He walked back to the car and got in. Makda was almost frantic as she wondered what was about to happen.

He drove the car forward to where Makda was sitting beside the sick woman. Sitting in the car for thirty seconds, it was obvious a battle was taking place. Then Haji got out of the car and opened the trunk. Retrieving a sandwich and a cold bottle of water, he brought them to the woman who weakly smiled. Reaching a thin hand forward she grasped the bottle. She tried, to no avail, to twist off the bottle cap. Haji took the bottle from her hand, opened it and tilted it to her lips.

She coughed as the first swallow of cold water entered her mouth. Then she took another. And another.

Makda detected a small smile on Haji's face and thought to herself, 'Ah, God is good all the time'!

As they got back into the car, they saw the woman gently unwrapping the sandwich. She gave a weak wave and smile as the car pulled back onto the road.

Two hours later Haji turned east onto a dirt road. Fifteen minutes later, Haji said, "We'll stop here. After dark I'll lead you to a trail that'll take you across the Saudi border.

"When you're across, a friend of mine will drive you to Riyadh and to your new home with the Khalil's."

Makda said, "I have a really hard time believing anything you say."

Haji looked at her and said, "I'm telling you the truth. Makda, I really don't want anything bad to happen to you. If you follow my instructions, you'll be okay. I'll be with you when we meet my friend at the border. I'll make sure he understands he needs to get you safely to Riyadh."

He opened the trunk and retrieved sandwiches and bottles of water. Putting two bottles and two sandwiches in a bag for later, they ate and watched quietly as the sun set in the west.

When it was fully dark, Haji said, "It's time. Let's go."

Almost immediately they heard an explosion.

He remarked casually, "Well, there goes another one."

Makda, still shaken by the nearby blast, asked, "What do you mean?"

"Since earlier this year, the Saudi's and Yemeni's have been fighting. There've been a lot of battles fought and some were right where we're standing. As a result of troops coming and going across the border, mine fields have been put in place. If someone doesn't know where they are, they'll trip a mine. What we just heard was one of those mines being tripped by an Ethiopian looking for paradise in Saudi Arabia. I think he found paradise a lot quicker than he expected."

Makda shuddered and said, "So, how do you know where the mines are?"

"I've done this so many times, I could do it in my sleep. Make sure you follow my footsteps and in fifteen minutes we'll meet Abdu at the border."

Haji produced a small flashlight to help navigate the trail. She was terrified as they continued on, but there were no more explosions. Abruptly he stopped, turned off his light and listened. Everything was quiet. He waited and she held her breath.

Then, off to the right a small light blinked three times. Still they waited. Then, again, the light flashed four times and Haji said, "That's my friend Abdu."

Approaching one another carefully, the two embraced. They were friends separated by an invisible border yet joined by an illegal bond. Makda was a commodity, a pawn, an income-generator for many people in an efficient and well-oiled piece of trafficking machinery.

She reached in her backpack and grabbed a small Bible and gave it to Haji and said, "I've underlined some verses for you. Read them. If you're as sensitive and bright as I think you are, you'll read them and more importantly, you'll change your life. If you don't care about others, give the Bible to someone who will appreciate it. But, if you do give it away, remember you've thrown away the greatest treasure anyone could ever have."

Abdu and Makda made their way on a faint trail through the sand and scrub brush. Scared to death, she delicately stepped in Abdu's footprints. Fifteen minutes later they arrived at a parked car. They got in and soon were driving northwest.

After another ten minutes, they pulled onto a highway going north. Abdu said, "You may as well rest. We have a nine hour drive. If all goes well, I'll have you with the Khalil family by dinner-time this evening."

By mid-afternoon, they'd entered the southern part of Riyadh. Makda marveled at the cleanliness. Though Addis Ababa had skyscrapers, they would be dwarfed by the architecture of Riyadh.

Abdu said, "Makda, there's a few things you should know before I take you to the Khalil's. Saudi Arabia is an Islamic country. I saw you give a Bible to Haji. If you would do that in Saudi Arabia, you would be arrested, possibly tortured, likely get a lashing and would be imprisoned. If you were fortunate, you'd be deported.

"The Saudi's take their religion very seriously. Hundreds of people are employed throughout the country to try and convert foreign visitors to Islam.

"If you were successful in converting someone from Islam to Christianity, it would be considered apostasy for them and they'd be put to death.

"There's even a law that identifies all atheists as terrorists. To not believe in Allah or Islam has all kinds of consequences. I'm sure the Khalil family will give you all the information you need. If you did something illegal, immoral or wrong while working for the family, it reflects on them as well."

Then he continued, "We need to stop somewhere, get you cleaned up and into some nicer clothing."

Looking at Makda, Abdu said, "I know your trip has been long and hard. I'm not exactly sure what you're thinking right now, but you're safe. The Khalil family will treat you well."

Abdu parked the car near a large store, and asked Makda to wait for him. After ten minutes he emerged with three packages which he placed on the back seat.

The next stop was a large restaurant.

Parking the car, he said, "Bring the packages and we'll go inside for coffee. You can use the restroom to change your clothing and shoes. There's also a package of toiletry stuff so you can get cleaned up."

After ordering coffee and a pastry, Makda went to the restroom and locked the door. Looking at herself in the mirror she saw a sad, grubby young woman in dirty clothing. She washed herself as much as possible and changed her clothing. Throwing her old clothing into the trash can she looked in the mirror again. Though she looked and felt better, she thought she'd aged five years in the last two weeks.

When she arrived at the table, she saw her coffee and pastry. Abdu looked at her and said, "Ah, much better. You've cleaned up well."

Embarrassed, Makda began eating the pastry.

"We'll be at the Khalil's home in about an hour. Do you have any questions for me?"

Makda asked, "What can you tell me about the family?"

"I've not met them yet, but I've read the paperwork about them. Ammar is the husband. He's an architect and designs some of the buildings in Riyadh. His wife is Hija. They have three children. Their daughters are eight-year-old Esraa and two-year-old Haifa. Their only son is Asad who is six years old.

"The family's wealthy and are looking forward to having your help. You'll be doing domestic work for them as well as caring for their children.

"You need to know there'll be an expectation from the family to convert to Islam. But, there's no law demanding it.

"If you're caught publicly practicing Christianity, the penalties would be severe. Saudi law says non-Muslims are free to practice their faith privately. But, there are no guidelines in the law to identify private from public. So it's up to the discretion of the courts to determine whether you've violated the law or not. You should know things don't go in favor of non-Muslim people in Saudi Arabia. If you were Muslim, life would be much easier for you."

They finished their coffee and pastry and walked to the car. They drove through an obviously wealthy neighborhood and Abdu stopped outside a large gated home.

There was a high white wall surrounding the home with a large fabricated see-through steel gate with intricate designs. The home had three levels. It was spotless white with aqua trim on the corners and eaves. Makda asked Abdu, "Would you call this a mansion?"

"Ha. Yes. I'd call this a mansion! This is your new paradise."

A guard approached the gate and asked for information. Abdu replied in Arabic and the gate opened.

Driving around a circular driveway he stopped at steps leading up to a large veranda and porch. Makda marveled at the beauty. She'd thought a home couldn't get any better than Subira's, but she'd certainly been wrong.

A woman emerged from the front door. She was slim, young and smiling. Coming down the steps, she introduced herself as Hija. Just then three children came down the steps behind her. She noticed a boy, then an older girl carrying a much younger girl. Abdu introduced Makda to the family.

She felt incredibly disadvantaged in not understanding the Arabic conversation. Her confidence grew and her fears subsided as she saw the warm and genuine smiles on the faces of the family.

She didn't know how she was to greet them. In her own country she'd have kissed each one on the cheek but what did they do in Saudi Arabia?

Since no handshakes or kisses were initiated from them, she decided to watch and wait. As they went up the steps, Abdu and Makda followed. He leaned over and whispered, "Saudi women don't greet strangers in any way other than a 'hello'. You're wise in just waiting for others to show you their ways."

Entering the home, everyone removed their shoes. Makda stopped and looked. There was a magnificent, wide staircase made of marble going up to the second floor. The room she was in was huge and elegant. It was obvious this family was wealthy. Abdu had told her on the way to Riyadh that 'oil' had made the country rich and it was among the wealthiest nations in the world.

Looking at the home, she was getting a quick lesson about wealth. Her mind rapidly went to the poor people walking from Ethiopia to Djibouti and from Yemen to Saudi Arabia. They were risking their lives and all their possessions for a simple hope of finding a meager job in Riyadh. Makda felt a fleeting glimmer of shame as she stood in wonder at what was before her and the contrasting difference of the poverty she'd seen on the trip.

Then, her awe was disrupted by a man entering the room. Dressed impeccably in a black suit, Ammar joined the group. Abdu translated for him as he welcomed Makda to his home. He motioned to a maid to take Makda to her quarters.

Following the maid, she walked through a magnificent dining room, a kitchen, a pantry which you could actually walk through and finally down a hallway with several doors. The maid opened a door on the right. Makda walked into a small but comfortable room with a sofa, chair, table and bed. Through another door she saw a small bathroom with a shower.

The maid shut the door and left. Makda sat on the bed with her backpack beside her. Reaching into the backpack she retrieved her Bible. She'd given the last one of her pastor's twenty-four Bibles to Haji. Based upon what Abdu had said, she was thankful she didn't have any more to pass out. She didn't need that kind of trouble. Then she felt ashamed of her brief encounter with selfish thoughts.

Reality pushed aside the momentary guilt as she understood the implications of sharing the Gospel with others in Saudi Arabia. Though only seventeen, she'd devoted her life to 'learning the Gospel message', but more importantly she'd been taught 'how to live the Gospel'. She knew there was a profound difference.

Slowly, she realized she was in a perfect place to live the Gospel and hoped that others would notice.

Makda knelt beside her bed, with her Bible in her hands and prayed. *'Lord, You've brought me to this place. You're everywhere so I know You're here with me. Give me the courage, joy, peace and smiles so others can see my faith. I pray somehow, someway You'll let me be an ambassador for You. I'm afraid, but at the same time I'm excited. I thought You'd brought me to this place for a job. But* now I know what my real job is. Protect me and bless me. In Jesus' name, Amen'.

Methodically, Makda stood up and placed her Bible in the drawer of the nightstand beside her bed.

It was then she remembered what her pastor had said when he gave her the Bibles.

"When I look at the New Testament, I'm always amazed how the followers of Christ took His Gospel message to the world. Those men and women were scattered like 'seeds in the wind' and they took His Word wherever they went. You never know where God will take you, but one thing's for sure, He'll go with you wherever you go. Hide His Words in your hearts and you'll always have them when you need them."

She walked to the door.

She hesitated.

She grasped the doorknob and twisted.

The door opened.

Makda stepped confidently and bravely into a life God was going to use and bless.

PART 4

Maya and Lola's New Life

September 2015 - September 2019

Chapter 15

Addis Ababa, Ethiopia - Monday, September 21, 2015

Maya

SHE wondered if the professional young man in the suit and tie who picked her up at Subira's worked for the textile factory or if he was simply her delivery man.

Maya turned her head slightly to see her driver looking at her. She quickly glanced out her window to avoid an inevitable conversation. But it was to no avail as he asked, "How old are you?"

Quietly, Maya replied, "Thirteen."

"I'm sorry, what did you say?"

"I'm thirteen."

"Oh. I have a sister who's thirteen." He smiled and asked, "Where did you come from?"

Maya was annoyed. He was young, yet trying to make himself look older by wearing a suit and tie. Maybe if she didn't answer his questions, he'd be quiet.

Then, the politeness instilled by her mother rose to the surface and she answered, "From a village in the western highlands."

Even though it'd only been fifteen minutes since she left Subira's, she was already missing the other girls, especially her cousin Lola with whom she'd travelled to Addis. Lola was a year younger and would become a domestic worker for an Addis family. Maya wondered if she'd ever see her cousin again.

The six girls at Subira's had developed a bond akin to that of sisters. It was no small thing when one of them, Hana, had disappeared. Maya still got a knot in her stomach as she wondered what possibly could have happened to her.

"I said, do you have any brothers or sisters?"

Looking at the young man and realizing her daydreaming had distracted her, Maya decided to simply respond with a nod of her head.

He made a turn onto a side street and then into an industrial park. Maya saw many older brick buildings in desperate need of repair. The car stopped in front of one of the buildings which had four stories. He exited the car and she followed with her backpack. Walking through a door, they climbed a staircase to the third floor.

The young man opened a door and Maya was stunned as she saw a huge open area with possibly a hundred cots. They weaved through the many aisles between the cots until he pointed to an empty one and simply said, "This one is yours."

Placing her backpack on the bed she asked, "Now what?"

"The girls will be returning at six o-clock this evening from their shift. They work from six in the morning until six in the evening. The girls on the second floor work the alternate twelve hours."

Maya quickly responded, "Twelve hours! That's half a day!"

He laughed and said, "Yeah, you're right."

Sarcastically he continued, "You're a bright young lady, aren't you? Go ahead and get some rest until the girls return. You'll begin your shift tomorrow morning."

With that said, he left.

Maya wandered through the aisles of neatly made, tidy cots. There was nothing of value showing anywhere other than a washcloth and towel on the end of each bed.

Wandering to the windows, she peered into the industrial landscape below. It was a desolate view punctuated by forlorn, rusted pieces of machinery.

Going to her cot, she laid down. Her mind soon took her back to the coffee plants in the highlands which of course brought memories of her family. She wondered if her parents had any idea of what they'd committed their daughter to. How could they know? They had expectations she'd be providing support to their family while simultaneously creating a bright future for herself.

The noise of the returning girls suddenly woke her. Sitting up she watched as more and more girls filed into the large dormitory. Soon the cots were filled. There were inquisitive looks as several girls noticed the newcomer.

Finally, the girl in a cot next to Maya's, smiled and said, "Hi, my name's Elizabeth. What's yours?"

"Maya."

"It looks like we'll be neighbors."

Maya looked at the young woman who seemed to be a few years older than herself. "How long have you been here?"

"Next month it'll be three years."

"I can't imagine! Three years? How can you work twelve hours a day for three years?"

"Oh, we get one day off a week. That helps."

Maya frowned and said, "I don't think I'll be able to do that!"

Elizabeth whispered, "Maya, don't say that. If the management heard you say something like that, it wouldn't go well for you."

Subdued, Maya felt a darkness settling into her soul.

~~~~~~~~~~

Eight Months Later...

Maya looked at Elizabeth and said, "I asked my boss today if there was a chance I could get a management position sometime."

"What did he say?"

"He said, 'maybe someday'. He told me I was doing a great job in running my loom and he didn't want to see my talent wasted at a desk.

"Before I came here, I was told my personality and perfectionism would probably get me into management. It doesn't look like that's going to happen."

Elizabeth noticed the familiar dark aura settling on her young friend once again. "Maya, you're going to have to accept where you're at or you're going to torment yourself to death!"

"I can't help it. At home in the mountains, my cousin Lola and I were free to come and go as long we finished our work. I'm only fourteen and I'm already feeling like an old woman. No family, no free time... just work, work and more work!"

Elizabeth stared at her and said, "Maya, you don't have anywhere to go. You don't know how to get home. You don't have a phone number for your aunt. Your money is accumulating in the factory's account. You don't have a choice."

With determination, Maya quietly said, "There are always choices."

~~~~~~~~~~

Four Months Later...

Maya sat on the curb, staring at the mud puddle between her feet. As the tears dripped from her chin, they created ripples when they hit the brown water.

Two nights ago she'd said goodbye to Elizabeth and three other co-worker friends. She'd had enough! The streets of Addis had to be better than the never-ending, back-breaking work and the lack of hope she'd felt at the factory. The contrast between her free life of peace in the highlands and the hard work in the dark and damp factory was more than she could handle. She'd simply left the dorm, descended the stairs and walked into a dark and starlit night.

She'd found herself at a dead-end when she realized there'd be no better position at the factory than what she had. There was no access to the supposed money accumulating for her in some inaccessible account. To top it off, the twelve hour shifts, six days a week had taken a physical toll. She was tired... horribly tired.

Now, on the street, she wondered if she'd made a mistake. At the factory, she at least had food and a bed. There, she'd also had friends. Now, alone, the doubts came. What had she done?

Standing up, she looked at the sun and realized it was noon. The horrible hunger was stirred once again as she caught a brief aroma of cooking food and realized how hungry she'd become. Moving up the street she saw a street vendor selling injera and beef. Approaching the elderly woman she asked, "Madam, could you spare a little bit of food for me?"

The woman turned to face Maya. A toothless grin on a wrinkled face offered hope, but the grin quickly disappeared and the words were harsh, "Ah, I see the rats are out again! Go away!"

Maya continued walking and saw a café. The door was open but she knew she shouldn't enter. Walking around the building she startled a dog nosing through the accumulated garbage alongside the building. Growling as she approached, the dog reluctantly gave ground and decided to leave.

Hesitant, though driven by necessity, she approached the foul-smelling trash. She found several half-eaten pieces of bread which she quickly ate. Finding nothing else edible she once again went to the street searching for another café or possibly a more generous street vendor.

The day wore on and her mind was filled with memories of her family and the mountains. Those were quickly pushed aside by the questions and concerns of her growling and cramping stomach. Then thoughts of her cousin Lola flooded in once again. Where was she? Did she get a good job? Would she ever see her again?

"Watch where you're going!"

Startled, Maya quickly moved to the side as a man on a bicycle narrowly missed hitting her.

The next forty-eight hours were a blur. Her mind felt like an artist's canvas covered in grey and black splotches of paint with no focus or purpose.

Wandering the streets of Addis Ababa was tiresome but she'd just found some more bread and a half bottle of water behind another café. She was finding her way around the alleys and streets of the capital city. The sun had set three hours earlier and she knew she needed to get to her 'nest'.

The night before she'd found a bakery on a side street. Behind the building she'd found bread crusts and more importantly a pile of wooden pallets and cardboard. With the breeze bringing the sweet smell of baking bread, the cardboard covering her small body and the pile of pallets getting her off the hard, damp ground, she'd slept better than at any other time in the past months. She began feeling just a little bit of joy in her new-found freedom.

Now, she found the right street and the smell of the bread pulled her forward. The street was dark except for a few flickers of light coming from various windows. Suddenly she heard a noise behind her and saw a man twenty feet away. The man was hurrying and soon he was beside her. Fearfully, she looked at him just as he struck her. Falling to the ground, she struggled as his strong hands picked her up as if she were a doll. Carrying her behind the bakery, he threw her on the ground.

She screamed again and again but no one responded to the cries of a fourteen-year-old girl from the western highlands of Ethiopia.

When the assault ended the man slinked away.

Chapter 16

Addis Ababa, Ethiopia - Monday, September 21, 2015

Lola

LEAVING Maya and the other girls behind at Subira's home was the most difficult thing Lola had ever done. The girls had become close. Each, having left their families, caused their friendships to flourish. When she'd left her family in the coffee highlands of western Ethiopia, it'd been hard, but this was immensely more difficult. She was alone.

Though she'd thought being twelve years old made her almost an adult, right now she was feeling more like a child.

When she'd left Subira's house, following the short and stocky woman to her car, she'd glanced over her shoulder and saw her smiling cousin Maya waving. That brought tears.

While driving through the streets of Addis Ababa, Lola tried to convince herself everything was going to be fine. After all, she would soon be living with a family and responsible for caring for their children. She'd be paid for doing something she loved. She also knew Maya would be making good money working in a factory. Hopefully, soon they would both be back with their families in the highlands.

The car stopped in front of a walled compound. Lola dutifully followed the matronly woman to the front gate. After knocking, a man emerged from the home and walked toward the gate. Lola saw a woman holding a baby with two children in the doorway.

With a huge smile, Mr. Tesfaye said, "Welcome, welcome! We've been looking forward to this day!"

Lola couldn't help but smile as she saw the children and felt the genuine welcome from their father.

Madame Tesfaye gave Lola a welcoming hug as the baby was squished between them. The baby smiled and Lola's heart melted.

"Our baby's name is Elizabeth and she's six months old." Pointing to the two shy children hiding behind their father, she continued, "These are our twins. The girl is Meti and the boy's name is Jonas. They're five years old. We're really happy to have you join our family."

~~~~~~~~~~

Twelve Months Later...

Lola laughed at the twins as they opened and closed an umbrella as if it were a new-found toy.

"Jonas! Be careful you don't poke Meti. That could hurt!"

Elizabeth had begun walking about five months earlier and was constantly exploring. Watching her, Lola smiled as she thought about how much she loved this family. Though missing Maya as well as their families back in the highlands, this job had not disappointed her. The Tesfaye family had been very kind to her and they permitted her to save her salary. It had been steadily accumulating in a sock in a drawer in her own bedroom and she was feeling blessed. When she felt the warmth of a blessing, it always prompted a thought of a verse or two Makda had told her to underline in her Bible. This time St. John 14:1 came to her mind. *'Don't let your heart be troubled. You believe in God, believe also in me'.*

Lola heard a noise as the front door opened and Mr. Tesfaye entered the room. The twins ran to their dad followed by a waddling Elizabeth.

"Lola, I hope you had a good day. It looks like my kids have been well taken care of!"

"Yes. It's been a busy one. You and Madame have some very active kids!"

He smiled as his wife came down the stairs from the second floor. Giving her a light kiss on her cheek, he said, "Lola, could you keep the children busy for a while? I'd like to have a coffee with my sweetie."

"Sure. That's why I'm here!"

They disappeared into the kitchen and Lola turned her attention to the energetic trio.

After dinner, Lola read a few stories to the twins. Elizabeth was already asleep as she tucked Jonas and Meti into their beds.

She entered the family room to tell the parents good-night. Mr Tesfaye said, "Lola, there's something I need to share with you."

Sitting down, Lola felt a heaviness as she noticed the seriousness on his face. Glancing at Madame, she noticed the same concerned look.

"As you know, I'm a Civil Engineer for a large company. Today I was informed they're moving our family to Abu Dhabi in the United Arab Emirates. I'm joining a new branch office they're opening there." Pausing, he continued, "I'm afraid we won't be able to take you with us. We're unable to get a passport and visa for you."

Lola was silent as a numbness crept its way into her body and mind.

Seeing the concern on her face, he quickly tried to reassure her, "You've been a huge part of our family and we don't know what we'd have done without you. We'll miss you very much but you don't have anything to worry about. With the money you've been saving, you'll have a good start for the future. I've found a great family for you to work for, so you'll be able to keep doing what you're so good at... taking care of kids. We'll be leaving in two weeks."

Lola, visibly sad, said, "Thanks for letting me know." Hanging her head she said, "I'll miss your family too. Is the new family one I can trust will treat me okay?"

"We don't know them, but we've done a lot of checking and we've been told they're fine people." Then he laughed as he said, "I'm sure they're not as fine as us, but maybe they'll be second-best. I'm sure you'll love them and they'll love you."

As she crawled into her bed that night, she couldn't help but worry. Then she remembered the words from Isaiah 41:10 – *Do not fear, for I am with you; do not be dismayed, for I am your God. I will strengthen you and help you; I will uphold you with my righteous right hand.*

Maya smiled as she remembered Makda and her insistence to memorize verses in the Bible.

Sleep didn't come quickly that night but eventually the peace of the Bible verse overcame the concerns for the future.

~~~~~~~~~

16 Days Later...

Saying good-bye to the Tesfaye family two weeks earlier had been more difficult and sad than she could have imagined. The children cried as they hugged Lola one last time.

Mr. Tesfaye had introduced her to the man who would deliver her to her new family. She turned to wave to the Tesfaye's as she climbed into the man's car.

Even now, two days after leaving the home, she couldn't believe what had happened next. After leaving the Tesfaye family, they drove for twenty minutes when the driver pulled his car to the curb. The man had grabbed Lola's backpack and said, "Let's see what you have in here."

Lola pulled on the strap and said, "No! That's mine! What are you doing?"

Raising his hand to strike her, she reluctantly released the pack holding all of her possessions in the world. Pulling out the items one by one, he laid them on the seat between them. Then, triumphantly, he grabbed a stuffed sock and said, "Hmm, I wonder what we have in here?"

Opening it, he held a fat wad of currency. Quickly he put it in his pocket and stuffed the rest of the items back into her pack. Handing the pack to her, he said, "You can take your things and get out."

"What do you mean?"

"Go!"

"What about the family I'm supposed to work for?"

With a smirk he answered, "I'm sure they'll find someone else. They don't know me and the Tesfaye's are almost gone. Go!"

Lola began crying as reality began to settle in, "I can't go without my money. That's everything I've earned this past year. I've worked hard for it."

"Well, it looks like you're going to learn about life the hard way. Go! Leave! Disappear!"

"Where can I go? I don't know anyone! I don't even know where I'm at!"

"You're in downtown Addis Ababa. I'm sure you'll make do." Then with a smirk he said, "A young girl like you can always find ways to make money."

Reaching over Lola, he opened her door and shoved her out. With a painful thud, she fell to the ground. He pulled the door shut and quickly drove away.

Now, two days later she was hungry and afraid. She'd slept on the street and was incredibly thankful for the sandwiches and packs of crackers the Tesfaye's had given her. But now her food and money were both gone... along with her hope.

Sitting with her back against a brick building and clutching her backpack, she closed her eyes. The warm afternoon sun bathed her face and soon she dozed.

Startled by a voice, she opened her eyes to see several boys and girls surrounding her. Quickly standing she looked at the group. They were dirty and their clothing was tattered. One of the girls grabbed her backpack. Lola couldn't resist. What could she do against them?

Opening the pack, the girl squealed as she pulled out a pair of socks. "Look, here's something I've not had for a few months!"

Soon the group had the backpack emptied and began walking away. Lola's shoulders drooped as she watched them leave. Then, one of the boys, the tallest of the group, turned around and looked at her. He said, "Well, you might as well grab your empty pack and come with us. You can't stay out here by yourself!"

Lola followed the group. A shorter boy dropped back to walk alongside her and asked, "What's your name?"

Reluctantly she replied, "Lola."

"Okay, that's a start. My name is Kaleb."

"Where are we going?"

"Oh, you'll see soon enough. But Ebo was right when he said you can't stay out here alone."

Fifteen minutes later, the group arrived at a dirt path winding its way between two large and dilapidated buildings. They entered one of the buildings through a broken-down opening that at one time must've been a doorway. Climbing an unstable wooden stairway, they emerged onto the second floor. Lola looked around and saw wooden pallets, trash and cardboard scattered here and there.

Kaleb said, "Come over here. There's a place next to where I sleep."

Lola followed. She felt hopeless. The loss of her year's wages was staggering. She'd counted on it to get back to her family and provide them with the much needed income they were expecting. The loss of money, the betrayal of the man who should have delivered her to another family, the sadness of not being with the Tesfaye family, all brought her to tears. Looking down at the pallet and tattered cardboard, she thought of the soft mattress, pillow and clean sheets she had at the Tesfaye's just two days earlier. How was it possible her life could have changed so much and so quickly?

"Do you like it?"

She looked up at Kaleb through blurred and tear-filled eyes and replied numbly, "Thanks, but you have no idea where I've come from or you wouldn't have asked me that question."

Quickly he said, "I'm sorry. I didn't mean anything by it."

"I really did mean it when I said thanks. I knew I couldn't stay on the streets. This is a lot better than that!"

Sitting down on the pallet she looked around the room, wondering whether this rag-tag bunch was her new family. She wondered what price she'd need to pay for the security and safety this gang would provide.

The days and nights came and just as quickly disappeared as the gang continually scoured the streets of Addis. Searching for anything they could use, eat, steal or sell, they were experts at surviving.

Lola couldn't help but compare her current life with that of the Tesfaye family. She likewise couldn't stop the flow of thoughts about her previous life in the mountains as they barged their way into her mind. As the weeks and months went by, her mind drifted less and less to the mountains and her family.

But, she couldn't help wondering what happened to her cousin Maya. She knew Maya was a survivor and able to solve any problem she faced. She smiled as she pictured Maya sitting behind a desk managing a textile business. Then she laughed out loud as she remembered Maya was only 14 or 15 years old.

"What's so funny?"

Lola looked at the tall, thin Ebo and said, "Nothing. I just had a memory of my cousin."

Ebo responded, "Don't be thinking too long about your past. You have a new life and need to focus on what to do to help the rest of us. You've gotta do your part."

Lola nodded and kept walking. Seeing Kaleb ahead of her she broke into a run.

Hearing the footsteps behind him, he turned and grinned.

Kaleb and Lola had become close friends. They spent their free time together and silence wasn't part of their relationship. They talked about everything.

He'd told his story to her several months earlier. He'd been from a family of nine children in southeastern Ethiopia. His father was killed in a truck accident and quickly his mother sent Kaleb to Addis to find work. Her ability to care for the remaining eight children was dismal at best. Without Kaleb's income she knew she'd be incapable of caring for her remaining children. He worried about what had become of them as he'd been unable to find work and send funds back to her. At least his mom had one less mouth to feed.

Living alone on the streets, he quickly found his way into Ebo's gang. At first he tried desperately to honor his father and mother's Christian religion of 'not stealing', but soon there was no choice. He became adept at snatching purses, wallets, and suitcases from tourists too intent on what they were buying in the market.

Whatever the gang members found or stole had to come to the communal coffers of Ebo's gang. There it was shared. If anyone kept anything for themselves and was discovered, they'd suffer a violent beating from Ebo. If it happened twice, they received another beating and were physically removed from the gang.

As girls were brought into the gang, they were quickly 'claimed' by one of the male gang members. He became their protector. Kaleb made it known on the first day that he was Lola's 'friend'. That made her untouchable to the others and added security to her.

Now, while lying on their individual cardboard beds, she remembered their memorable 'friendship' conversation months ago. Kaleb had said, "Lola, there's something I want to tell you."

Looking at him in the dim moonlight, she waited.

Hesitating, he said, "I really like you Lola and I want you to know you're safe with me. But, I'm not going to have a relationship with you like you see with others in our gang. My mother and father taught me right from wrong and more importantly showed me in the Bible what God thought about certain things. I just wanted you to know what I believed so you didn't have to worry about me." He continued, "Besides, you're only thirteen and since I'm seventeen, I'm almost an old man compared to you."

Lola had breathed an audible sigh of relief then and said, "I was raised as a Muslim and grew up believing some wrong things about Christians and their Book. I had a friend who gave me a Bible and shared verses with me which have become important. Through it all, I'm learning more about Allah or God. Kaleb, I like you very much too and I thank God you're a friend I can trust. Right now, I'm not sure what I'd do without you."

Kaleb had responded, "I'm not sure how much longer I'll stay in Addis. I think I'd like to find my family in the south. It's been way too long and I'm getting really tired of the city life. A lot of poor country people think Addis is paradise, but you and I know different."

That conversation had been a huge blessing to her as she was feeling much safer as a result of their friendship. More importantly, they were able to study the Bible together and learn what God's plan might be for the future.

Now, a year and half later, Lola was learning more and more about God's love, grace, mercy, peace and salvation.

As a Muslim, she was raised to believe Allah had no family. By reading the Bible she was surprised to learn Christians believed God was a Father and had a Son named Jesus. That was just as astounding as learning God was also a Spirit living inside her.

She'd been taught that the greatest sin in Islam was worshipping any Gods other than Allah. As a Muslim, she'd believed Allah alone is God and had no family. So, the thought that God was the Father of Jesus and was also a Spirit was confusing. The concept of worshipping the Father, Son and Holy Spirit was called 'shirk' in Islam, and she felt incredibly repulsed at the thought of Christianity... yet drawn toward it at the same time.

The confusion prompted a question, "Kaleb, this life is horrible. Living like we do every day and stealing for food is a terrible way to live. Being separated from my family and my cousin Maya is awful. There's absolutely nothing in my life that can be called 'good'."

Faking a sad face, he said, "Nothing? Not even me? I'm not a good thing?"

"Ha. You know what I mean. You're the only good thing. But, what I was going to say is there's almost nothing in my life today or tomorrow that's encouraging or good. But, in spite of all the 'bad', I feel peaceful inside. That's impossible to imagine or even explain. How can that be?" Then quietly she asked, "I know the Bible says that God's Spirit is a 'comforter', so is what I'm feeling inside, God's Spirit?"

Kaleb smiled and said, "Let me show you something." He pulled his small New Testament from under his burlap pillow and flipped through the pages and said, "In Philippians 4:7, it says *'And the peace of God, which surpasses all understanding, will protect your hearts and minds through Christ Jesus.'*"

He continued, "The peace you have in your heart is beyond your understanding. That's why you have a hard time describing it."

Pausing, he looked at her and said, "When life is hard and I'm feeling more peaceful than I should be, I know it's God's Spirit giving me comfort."

With a questioning look, Lola asked, "How can you be sure it's God's Spirit giving you the peace?"

"Believe me. I've been around a lot of wicked people and I know the difference. Watch what happens to people who don't have God's Spirit inside them. When bad things happen, they fall apart. Many become violent or angry, lash out at others and begin to blame. But, if you watch people, you'll see some actually become better people because of their circumstances rather than becoming evil. That's the reason you said, 'In spite of all the bad, I feel peaceful inside.'"

Lola replied, "That scares me. If I say God has a Spirit, I'm guilty of what the Islamic Quran calls shirk."

"What you're feeling inside isn't something you've been taught or something someone has forced you to believe. It's something supernatural and it's a free gift God's given you. You don't need to fear anything God gives you. The Bible says that 'God is love.' He won't put anything evil inside you. If He wants to give you peace and comfort, accept it."

Turning some more pages, Kaleb read from 1 John 4:18, *'There is no fear in love, but perfect love casts out fear, because fear has to do with punishment. Whoever fears isn't perfect in love.'*

Lola thought a few seconds and then said, "That makes sense. I think I'll start watching how people react when they have trouble in their lives." Pausing again, she said, "Maybe you and I are placed here with our friends, just to help them learn about God? What do you think?"

"I've always wanted to share the Bible with them, but I was alone. Now I know why Jesus sent the disciples out two by two."

Lola asked, "What do you mean?"

Laughing quietly Kaleb replied, "That's a subject for another time. Let's get some sleep."

Lola curled up, pulled up the rough burlap bag which still had a faint aroma of coffee beans, and peacefully went to sleep.

~~~~~~~~~~

A Year Later...

THE lion's mouth was open. His mane flowed magnificently. His tail arched over his back. Lola looked at him in awe.

He was cold, silent, unmoving.

Kaleb had told her the huge, bronze, Lion of Judah statue had been in front of the Addis Ababa Railway Station since 1930. It was created to be a symbol for 'change' in Ethiopia.

Yet, Lola wondered if things would ever change. She slowly walked to a bench near the statue and sat down in the shade of a large Eucalyptus tree.

The gang had spent most of the day in the area near the railway station to 'harvest' more food, handbags, cameras or whatever they could glean from unfocused and weary travelers.

She missed Kaleb. Two weeks earlier he'd decided to travel south to find his mother and siblings. When he left, her life changed. It wasn't good, progressive change like the bronze lion symbolized, but things had become even more difficult. No longer protected by him, other gang members were vying for her attention. She continually deterred them, but it was becoming more and more difficult.

She'd changed too. She was no longer the shy, twelve-year-old girl from the western highlands. She was now fifteen and in many ways had the emotional and physical strength of someone much older. Living on the streets of Addis produced a resilience not found elsewhere.

Yet, there was something spiritual that had changed as well. Her knowledge of the Bible and her gradual acceptance of Jesus Christ was giving her a huge hope for the future.

Taking a deep breath, Lola savored the minty, sweet, almost honey-like aroma of the towering tree above her.

It reminded her of the highlands forest where her family raised coffee plants. Would she ever see the forest or her family again? What about her best friend and cousin Maya? It'd been three years since she'd seen her. Maya had gone to the Addis textile mills at the same time Lola had become a domestic worker for the Tesfaye family.

Three years! A year with the Tesfaye's until he'd been reassigned to Abu Dhabi and then two years with the gang on the streets of Addis.

She thought, *'I wonder what my life would be like if I had...'*

Suddenly she was interrupted by someone saying, "Excuse me. I was asking if I could sit here beside you?"

Jolted from her thoughts, Lola said, "Oh, I'm sorry. Yeah, you can sit here. My mind was wondering and I was 500 miles away."

The woman smiled and sat down. "500 miles? Where is that, if I could ask?"

Lola smiled and said, "In the northwest highlands."

"Oh. I've never been there. Is it beautiful?"

Lola's face lit up as she said, "Yes! No tall buildings, asphalt, crowds, smog or exhaust fumes. Just family."

"What's your name?"

"Lola."

"My name is Sara. I'm happy to meet you."

Lola looked at her for a few lingering seconds. The woman was probably forty years old and seemed kind.

Though she needed to get back to the railway station soon, she felt drawn to this friendly, smiling woman. 'Normal' conversations with people didn't happen often and this was feeling good. She'd grown accustomed to looking at strangers as someone to steal from, but the woman's smile softened her heart. She reminded Lola of her mother. It'd be difficult to steal from this woman, but...

The conversation continued, yet Lola knew there'd be a price to pay if she returned empty-handed to Ebo and the gang. She eyed Sara's purse lying between the two of them. She casually shifted herself on the bench and placed her hand on the purse handle. Tensing, she continued listening to Sara as her fingers clasped the hard plastic handle...

Then Sara said, "I was just like you."

Lola looked at Sara and said, "What?"

"I was just like you. Living on the streets, part of a gang, taking advantage of strangers."

Sara looked directly into Lola's eyes and said, "I can give you something much more valuable than anything you'll find in my purse."

Lola looked down and casually removed her fingers and hand from the purse handle.

"What do you mean? You don't know anything about me."

Sara smiled and said, "Today isn't the first time I've seen you. It's my business to know the gangs in Addis. I've watched you for months. I know Ebo. I don't see Kaleb though. Has he gone back to his mother?"

Lola's mouth opened but no words came. She felt fear.

Sara said, "Don't be afraid. I have an organization that helps young people like you. Ebo has never wanted my help, though I've tried. Sometimes when someone's on the street for a long time, they prefer that kind of freedom instead of what I call 'real freedom.'"

She continued, "I've helped a lot of young women and men find 'real freedom' over the last few years. Only a fraction of those I've talked to accept my help." Looking intently at Lola, she asked, "What about you? Would you like to experience 'real freedom' in your life?"

Lola, with eyes full of mistrust, asked, "What do you mean? What would I have to do?"

Sara smiled and said, "Come with me. Right now. I'll have a bed for you, food to eat and a job."

Lola laughed out loud and said, "Believe me, I've been offered that many times before and you can see where it's taken me!"

"I understand. I've been there too. Twenty-three years ago, I was given a chance like I'm giving you."

Lola was startled when she saw Ebo and three others from her gang coming out of the railway station. Ebo stopped when he saw Lola. With quick strides he was soon standing over them.

With a smile, Sara said, "Good afternoon Ebo."

He acknowledged her, "Sara, haven't seen you for a while. Looks like you're up to your old tricks in trying to mess with my friends?"

Laughing, Sara responded, "You know I'd never take anyone away from you who doesn't want to come. In some ways, you and I are alike. We provide a safe place for vulnerable young people."

"I suppose that's true. Lola was in a really tough spot when we found her."

Then he looked at Lola and asked, "Has Sara given you her little speech about 'real freedom' yet?"

Pausing, Lola wasn't sure what to make of Ebo's and Sara's relationship. Then, she answered, "Yes. She has."

"Well... Sara's genuine. She can help you get started all over again... if that's what you want. You can trust her."

Lola, dumbfounded, replied, "Ebo, are you saying you want me to leave?"

"You know all of us love you. But with Kaleb gone, your life is only going to get worse. Besides, you know as well as I, there are a lot more kids we can bring into the gang. This is your choice. Most of us are at home on the streets, even though it's tough. If you go with Sara, you're going to learn about structure and hard work. But, maybe that's what you're really searching for. Looks like you have a choice to make."

Looking at Sara, he said, "Catch you later Sara. You take care of yourself and keep that purse held tight! I heard there's some desperate people in this area."

With a smile, Ebo began walking away. Lola looked at the retreating group of friends. They stopped at the entrance to the train station and watched Lola. The tug of the familiar was at war with the tug of the unknown.

She remembered a verse Makda had her memorize from Proverbs chapter 3. *'Trust in the Lord with all your heart; lean not on your own understanding. In all your ways, acknowledge Him and He'll direct your paths.'*

She looked at Sara and stood up. Running toward Ebo, the gang waited.

Sara stood and watched. What would happen next?

Lola hugged each of the group and returned to Sara with tear-filled eyes.

Standing together, Sara reached down and held Lola's hand, the one which had been wrapped around her purse handle. Together they watched the gang disappear into the station.

"Okay Lola. It looks like you've made your decision. Now, it's time to get you to 'real freedom'. Oh, did I tell you the name of our organization? It's called *'Real Freedom'*!"

With that, Sara laughed as they walked toward a car parked along a side-street.

~~~~~~~~~

A Year Later...

The workday was almost over when Sara said, "Lola, come with me."

She followed Sara to the large storage room at the *Real Freedom* offices.

"We're going to do something a little different today."

Lola had been busy the past year learning about all the things *Real Freedom* accomplished in Addis with their four main focus groups.

- Helping young men and women exit the street-life
- Working with young girls and women who worked the streets of night-time Addis
- Helping single mothers find employment and self-sufficiency
- Helping people from each group become part of a church fellowship group

"Tonight we're going to help some young mothers. Do you mind working some extra hours?"

Lola said, "No problem. I don't have anywhere else to go."

"Okay. Grab four of those large bags and we'll fill them with some things. Diapers, toys, toiletries and food. We'll take them to a place near Mercato."

Finally, they had the four bags stuffed into the car's backseat and trunk and made their way through traffic. The sun was setting as they pulled up to a large brick building. The run-down two story façade didn't seem very inviting.

Tugging the large bags out of the back seat and trunk, Sara and Lola went to a door at the front of the building. Climbing the stairs to the second floor was no easy task.

Arriving at the top, Lola gasped at the sight. Approximately a hundred children were in a wide open area. She noticed babies as well as kids up to eight years old. The noise! But it was a good noise. Even a baby crying was a refreshing sound!

A large woman approached and Sara said, "Nyala, it's good to see you! It looks like you haven't run out of work!"

Sara continued, "Oh, I want you to meet Lola. She's been working with me for a year, but this is the first time she's been here."

Lola placed her bags on the floor and hugged Nyala. "Welcome Lola. I'm sure you've learned a lot working with Sara."

Looking at the kids, she said, "There's a lot of girls and women who work nights on the streets and have nowhere to take their children. So, we take care of them here. As you can see, we're busy." And then with a huge smile, "If you get tired of working for Sara, come see me."

Sara laughed and said to Lola, "Nyala does a tremendous service for the women. Without her, these children would be in a really vulnerable environment."

"Come! Let me show you around. I have four girls helping with the children tonight. That makes five of us caring for almost one-hundred and fifty kids. That's a lot of diapers!"

Wending their way through the crawling infants, toys, bouncing balls and partitions, they continued the tour. It had been a long time since she'd seen children so happy.

As they neared the back wall, a young lady was feeding a bottle to a baby. She looked up and smiled at the passing group.

Lola gasped! "Hana?"

The girl stared and quietly said, "Lola?"

For a few seconds they looked at one another. Nyala took the baby Hana had been feeding and watched as Hana and Lola hugged for a long time.

Lola exclaimed, "It's been four years!"

Hana replied, "I don't... I don't know what to say!"

Lola, with tears, said "I can't believe it's you. You disappeared at the Mercato market four years ago and we never knew what happened to you. I've always thought the worst."

Hana said, "When I was at Subira's and we went to the market, a woman approached me and told me Subira was trafficking girls and I needed to get away. It took a few days, but I finally believed her. I live with the two girls who helped get me away from Subira and I've been working with Nyala for the last four years."

Lola replied, "I wish I could have gone with you. Life hasn't been easy for me." Then with another hug and huge smile, she added, "I think you and I have a lot to catch up on!"

Nyala and Sara were dumbfounded, watching the reunion in amazement.

Sara said, "Nyala, we'll have to make sure these girls get to spend some time together soon."

Chapter 17

Addis Ababa, Ethiopia – November 6, 2019

MAYA

"**MAMA,** I'm hungry."

Maya looked at her two-year-old daughter and said, "Let's see what we can do about that!"

Reaching under her small bed, she tugged at a box. Reluctantly it came out after a heavy yank. Opening it, Maya pulled out a small package of crackers.

Setting Lola Marie on her lap, she carefully opened the packet. Holding a cracker high in the air, she said, "Here it is."

Lola Marie stretched her arm into the air as she reached for it, but Maya kept it just a little higher. Finally, with a spurt, the cracker was in her hand.

"My little sweetie, I love you so much."

She remembered the fear she'd felt when she knew she was pregnant. She'd thought, 'I can barely take care of myself, what will I do with another mouth to feed'?

It had been a cold, rainy night when her contractions started, but thankfully two other women were willing to help with the delivery. Many babies were born to the women working the streets of Addis and she'd likewise helped others with their births. The life these babies were born into held little promise or hope for a bright future. Sadly, many of the children would follow their mother's vocation.

When she'd first looked at her baby, Maya prayed that God would bless her newborn with a good and long life. One of the mid-wives had asked, "What are you going to name your little girl?"

Without hesitation she answered, "I'm naming her Lola, after my best friend and cousin. I don't know that I'll ever see her again, so this name will help keep her memory alive."

And it had...

Maya thought about her years of working with her cousin Lola in the coffee groves of the highlands. They were sweet memories, but it had now been four years since she'd last seen her and it seemed so long ago. She hoped Lola was on a better path in Addis than she herself was experiencing.

But for now she had to concentrate on the tough situation she found herself in. Two-year-old Lola Marie was a handful and trying to keep her safe and close by when she was busy with a customer wasn't easy.

She remembered the traumatic day, seven months ago when she knew she was once again pregnant. She'd wept.

From her previous experience, she knew she had no choice but to continue working up to her second baby's delivery. Then, she'd quickly need to get back on the streets. There was no other way to pay the rent for her hut or for purchasing food. The rent, food and clothing meant Maya needed to work seven days a week, 365 days a year. There were no breaks or sick days. No vacation. No pregnancy leaves.

Of course, she wondered about her future. What if I'm stabbed or beaten? Who would take care of the kids? It wasn't uncommon for a drunk customer or one on drugs to take out their anger on a vulnerable girl or woman. Maya saw the scars on her friends.

What happens when I'm no longer 'pretty'? What if I'm arrested? What happens when I'm too sick to work? What if...?

The what-if's of her vocation created ongoing anxiety, stress and uncertainty. Then she remembered hearing that anxiety and stress could create physical illness. She felt hopeless. She felt helpless. The never-ending feelings of guilt and shame were in constant tension with her Biblical understanding of morality. It seemed she was trapped in a continuous circle of doom. It just didn't stop!

Sadly, she wondered how she'd be able to work with two children. When Lola Marie was born, she was able to keep her in the hut even when she had a customer. But that wasn't an option now that she was two years old. She had to trust that Lola Marie would be okay alone on the street outside her hut during those multiple times each night when Maya was busy.

It was then Maya knew she had no choice. She would need to pay someone to care for her two-year-old each night.

Later that afternoon Maya recognized a woman walking toward her with two children. "Hey Mari. How are you and your kids doing?"

"Good to see you Maya. We're doing okay. How about you?"

Maya smiled and said, "I'm sure you know the answer to that question."

Reaching down, Mari ruffled Lola Marie's hair and said, "Hey sweetie, you sure are the pretty one."

"Mari, I have a question. I know you take your two kids to a woman who takes care of them. Since I'm pregnant, I'm needing to do something with Lola. Do you think your sitter would have room for one more?"

"Tell you what. I'm going there right now and I already know she won't turn anyone away. She'd take good care of Lola Marie if that's what you decide to do."

"It's almost impossible for me to quit worrying about her during the evenings. With another baby coming in two months, I should get her started with a sitter now rather than later."

Mari said, "You're in the same spot I was in a couple of years ago. I've never regretted taking them to a sitter. Now my worry is what I'll do with them when they're nine or ten. Oh well, there's always something to worry about, I suppose."

Maya didn't want to start thinking that far ahead. She had enough worries for today. Hesitant, she asked, "Could you take Lola Marie with you today?"

"Sure, but you'll need to give the lady forty birr for the night. Do you have that much?"

Maya disappeared into her tin hut and a minute later dropped the coins into Mari's hand.

Holding her hands out to Lola Marie, she said, "Hey baby girl, I'll see you in the morning. Come, give Mama a hug."

As she watched Mari walking away with the three children, Maya was silently thankful Lola Marie hadn't cried. She realized the two-year-old was already tough and resilient. She wondered if that was a good or a bad thing.

The next morning Mari brought Lola Marie home. The little girl's chatter indicated the excitement she'd had at the sitters. Maya felt sadness as she realized Lola Marie's world had just gotten bigger and she wasn't there to experience it with her.

She wondered if her sadness was how her own mother had felt when Maya had been taken to Addis at thirteen to work in the textile mills. It was probably the same emotion, it's just that it's happening so much sooner for little Lola Marie.

Working at night made it important to sleep during the day, so after eating some bread and cheese, the two laid down on their narrow mattress. Lola Marie quickly fell asleep, but the baby growing inside Maya kept kicking. She smiled at the life within her, in spite of the additional complexity the baby would bring to her already complex life.

Mid-afternoon, Lola Marie woke up. Her stirring immediately woke Maya. They washed, had a bite to eat and then took a walk around the neighborhood.

The streets were littered with garbage, empty water bottles, and plastic bags. The only thing missing were garbage containers. Maya knew there were elegant streets in other areas of Addis and they were spotless compared to this. She also knew the government was rapidly cleaning up the dirty areas and moving people to new neighborhoods. As a result, girls like herself, working the streets, would need to find other places where their vocations would be tolerated. That was another uncertainty in her future. What if...?

She was always amazed at the number of girls and women in this area. They weren't apparent during the day because their doors were shut and most were sleeping. But at night it was different. If a person walked the night streets, they'd notice a door every ten to fifteen feet. The door was either shut, indicating 'busy', or a girl was standing in front of an open door. The huts were small. There was barely enough room for a small bed and cabinet. There were no chairs as the bed served many purposes. The women sat, ate and slept on the bed.

The streets were very dark as there were no street lights. But above some doors was a solitary, red-light bulb to attract attention. It seemed every block also had a bar with neon lights in the windows and muffled music escaping through the open door.

The sights and sounds were one thing. The sour, stale smells were another. Garbage and sewage removal were almost non-existent. It seemed infrastructure development stopped at the invisible lines marking these kinds of neighborhoods.

The men walking the night streets were interesting to watch. Many wore hoods or caps. Were they hiding? Ashamed? Their furtive and slinky postures almost made Maya laugh. They should be ashamed!

Arriving back at their hut, Maya and Lola Marie were hungry.

"Lola, what do you think? Do you want some injera?"

The little girl screamed "Yes!"

"Well, let's go find some."

They walked a block to an outdoor vendor who sold the injera. Served with a tomato based vegetable sauce, they couldn't wait to get it home. It wasn't often they splurged on something so good. Usually they ate bread, cheeses and sometimes mutton.

Soon, Mari arrived to pick up Lola Marie for the sitter... and another long and dreaded night began for Maya.

After climbing the stairs to the second floor, Mari looked around for Nyala. Not spotting her, one of the sitters noticed her and said, "Hi Mari. Nyala had to leave for a few minutes, but she'll be back soon. We ran out of diapers and that'd be a disaster in a big hurry!"

Mari laughed and said, "No problem Hana. Here are my two kids and I'm also dropping off a friends daughter."

She placed the birr notes into Hana's hands and said, "I'll see you in the morning."

"Thanks... oh, by the way, I know your two kids but what's the little girl's name?"

Mari said, "Her name is Lola Marie. She's two years old."

Hana smiled and said, "That's an unusual name. Now I know two Lola's."

"What do you mean?"

"I had a friend named Lola but I lost track of her about four years ago. Thanks, we'll see you in the morning."

Picking up the two year old, Hana said, "Lola Marie, my name is Hana. I'm your sitter today. Oh my, you're a pretty little girl. Let's go see what we can find for you to play with. I think you'll have fun with the other girls."

"Mari, you've been a huge help. Thanks for taking Lola Marie to the sitters for these past two weeks."

"That's no problem, I go there anyway. How does she seem after coming back?"

Maya answered, "I can tell she's getting a mind of her own. I'm guessing there's not a lot of discipline or structure there. But, from what you've said, they have a hundred and fifty kids to take care of."

"When you walk in, it seems like chaos. But the girls do a great job. They know what they're doing and they genuinely love the kids."

Maya responded, "It's probably time I start taking her there myself."

"Tell you what. Let's go together this afternoon. I'll introduce you to Nyala."

"I'd like that."

Maya took Lola Marie's hand and they walked the five blocks to the large, run-down building with Mari and her two children.

Opening the front door, they took the stairs to the second floor. Maya could sense the excitement in Lola Marie as the noise of the children above grew louder with each step they took.

Then, Maya saw the chaos! Children everywhere. But it was a good chaos. The area was well lit and sunlight, though dimming, was still filtering into the massive second floor room. She saw a few babies sleeping on blankets nearby and wondered how they could sleep amid the noise. Then she realized how quickly she herself had acclimated to life on the streets. Likely it was no different for the babies.

A woman approached Maya and introduced herself as Nyala. Lola Marie smiled at her sitter and held out her arms. Nyala picked her up and said, "Baby girl, now I know why you're so pretty. You look like your mama!"

"It's so good to meet you Maya! Lola Marie's getting along really good here with the other kids. She's never a problem. She shares toys and I don't think I've ever heard her cry in the two weeks she's been here. I'm sure you're proud of her."

"Oh, I am. I wondered if she... "

Nyala looked at Maya. "Maya, are you okay?"

But Maya simply whispered, "Hana... Hana... it can't be!"

Nyala turned to see Hana feeding a baby ten feet away. "You know Hana?"

"Yes! I do!"

Maya quickly covered the ten feet to an incredulous Hana. The two hugged for a very long time.

Hana said, "Maya, you're Lola Marie's mother?"

Barely able to answer, Maya simply said, "Yes... "

"I dearly love your little girl. She gets along really well here."

"Hana! I can't believe it. You're here, right now, with me, in this place! We thought you were gone forever when you disappeared at Mercato. We thought something really bad had happened to you."

They hugged again. Then Hana looked down at Maya's protruding stomach and said, "You're pregnant?"

Maya laughed and said, "Oh, I was keeping it a secret. How did you know?"

They both laughed.

Nyala interrupted and said, "Hana, I need to talk to you a minute and then we'll need to get back to work."

"Okay. Maya, I'll see you soon. I still can't believe it!"

They hugged and Maya and Mari disappeared down the stairway to another night of work.

Nyala looked at Hana with a smile and said, "I'm excited for you and Maya to find each other. That's really something that you've now been able to connect with two old friends."

Hana's mouth dropped open as she said, "Oh no! I was so excited to see Maya, I forgot to tell her about meeting her cousin Lola!"

Nyala said, "I know you forgot and that's why I wanted to talk to you. I've got an idea! Let's set up a surprise party for the three of you. Okay?"

With a smile, Hana said, "Oh, you have no idea what that would mean to me... and to them. That would be so much more than I could have ever hoped for. Yes. I would love that. You'd help me?"

"Of course. You can't imagine how this is getting me excited. God is really blessing you girls!"

Hana said, "Actually, now I'm feeling a little ashamed. I've been thinking about the coincidence of finding Lola and now Maya. But it's not a coincidence, is it?"

"No, there's no way it's a coincidence. Some people call it fate. You and I both know it's a God thing."

Nyala continued, "I'll need to talk to Sara over at *Real Freedom* to help make this happen. Maybe we can have the party at her offices. That'd be a lot nicer than here! Now, scoot... back to work you go!"

That afternoon, Nyala told Hana the reunion was all set for Saturday afternoon, just two days away.

"Neither Lola or Maya will know about each other until they get there. We'll tell each of them ahead of time that we want to set up a 'catching-up' time with you. Do you think that'll work?"

With tears in her eyes, Hana said, "All I can say is thank you. You have no idea what this will mean for the three of us. Thanks!"

"Let's see, this is Thursday, so you'll see Maya tomorrow morning and again on Saturday morning. You'll have to be careful to not let the secret out. I'll let Maya know about the party so you won't have to."

"Okay. No problem. I can keep secrets."

PART 5

Reunion

November 2019

Chapter 18

Addis Ababa, Ethiopia – November 23, 2019

"WHAT'S a party, Mama?"

Maya looked at her two-year-old daughter Lola Marie and replied, "It's a time you spend with friends laughing and having fun. Oh, usually there's a lot of good food to eat too."

Lola Marie smiled.

In the distance Maya could see the building where they were to meet Nyala and Hana. As she got closer she saw a large sign over a door that read "REAL FREEDOM".

Maya smiled as she read it. She recalled how Makda used to tell the girls at Subira's about Jesus Christ. Then she remembered a Bible verse as she stopped and re-read the sign... St. John 8:36 – *'If the Son sets you free, you'll indeed be free!'*

As she and Lola Marie walked through the doorway, Maya wondered if there was real freedom inside. She immediately saw a poster on a wall of Jesus holding a child on His lap.

There was a chair in the foyer so she sat down, not knowing where else to go. Surely someone would come soon.

A minute later, a woman entered.

The woman smiled and said, "You must be Maya? My name is Sara. Welcome to *'Real Freedom'*."

Maya stood and said, "Yes, I'm Maya and this is Lola Marie."

Stooping down, Sara said, "Lola Marie, you look like a really sweet little girl. Come, let's go find Hana and Nyala."

Entering a large room, Maya saw Hana talking to Nyala. Hana turned, noticed Maya and Lola Marie, quickly walked toward them and gave them hugs.

Lola Marie was excited to see Hana and Nyala. Her weeks at the child-care facility had been good weeks. It was obvious she loved her two sitters.

Maya looked around the room. There was a table with a birthday cake, cookies and other snacks.

"Whose birthday is it?"

Hana said, "I'll bet Lola Marie hasn't had her two year birthday party yet, has she?"

Maya hung her head and said, "No. Her birthday was six months ago and I'm not in a position to give her a party."

Laughing, Hana said, "Well, pretty soon we'll have a party for this two-year-old!"

Sara said, "C'mon girls. Let's sit down and catch up. I'm sure you two have plenty to talk about. Maya, I'm also looking forward to hearing your story. My organization is all about helping girls and women like yourself find real freedom."

There were six chairs in a circle. Maya sat Lola Marie on one of the chairs and the four women sat down.

Nyala said, "This is really an exciting thing for me. I'm surrounded by a lot of dark and ugly things in my neighborhood and this is absolutely the best thing I've seen in a long, long time! I'm thanking God that He's letting me be a part of this party!"

Then Sara said, "Oh, I'd like to have one of my *Real Freedom* employees join us. She needs to hear your stories too. I'll go get her and be right back."

Hana and Maya began talking. Hana could barely contain her excitement knowing the two cousins, Maya and Lola, would soon be reunited for the first time in four years.

Sara had made sure Maya was seated with her back to the door of the room. As she entered the room with Lola, Lola saw Hana and said, "Hey Hana... "

Maya's mouth immediately dropped open in confusion as she heard a familiar voice. Turning around she saw her best friend and cousin, Lola!

Lola recognized Maya at the same instant!

The distance between the two was covered in a split-second.

Maya and Lola hugged and cried together. Hana picked up Lola Marie when she began crying and said, "Everything's okay sweetie. Your mommy's crying happy-tears because she's excited to see her cousin."

So much had happened in the four years since they'd last seen each other. Both Maya and Lola had resolved themselves to the fact they'd likely never see each other again.

The next three hours were filled to the brim with laughter, tears, birthday cake, gifts and shock in learning about each other's lives. Soon, Hana, Lola and Maya had heard all the details of one another's past four years.

Then, Sara stood and walked to the table. Retrieving a small, wrapped gift, she gave it to Maya. It was a small box covered in a silver colored wrapping and a bright red bow. Carefully opening the box, Maya found a card. It simply said:

To Maya...
This card is your ticket to Real Freedom.
- Sara -

Looking at Sara, Maya said, "I don't understand..."

"It means what it says. I have a job for you. You can join us in helping girls and women like yourself find real freedom in their lives. You have so much first-hand experience you'd be a huge help to our organization. You'll be able to work alongside Lola. We also have our own child-care so Lola Marie can spend her days here too."

Maya silently cried, then stood and hugged Sara.

Then, all eyes were on Nyala as she stood and retrieved another wrapped gift from the table and handed it to Hana. "This gift is for you."

Unwrapping the gift, Hana read the card aloud:

> To Hana...
> Sara needs another child-care worker at Real Freedom.
> Though I desperately don't want to lose you,
> I know it'd be important for you to be with Lola and Maya.
> This is your ticket to Real Freedom.
> - Nyala -

Hana was stunned.

Then Lola broke the silence. Immediately, Maya knew the old Lola was back when Lola muttered with a mock frown, "Maya and Hana got presents today. I'm feeling pretty left out... "

Then with a smile she said, "But, the best present I could ever get is to be together with Hana and Maya again."

Picking up Lola Marie, she continued, "And it looks like the two Lola's will be getting to spend a lot of time together too! I'm still trying to figure out which of the two Lola's is prettier!"

Sara laughed at Lola's humor and said, "You know, I think there's something else we need to talk about. This reunion today reminds me of something important.

"Many times in life, bad things happen to good people and unfortunately, many innocent people suffer because of the actions of others. That tells us about the power of satan. But, what's happened here today is supernatural and talks about the power of God. He's brought the three of you together in a miraculous way. This reunion isn't a coincidence, it's an undeserved gift from God we call grace.

"We know God has unconditional love, great grace, mercy that's renewed every morning, indescribable peace and salvation. Those are all gifts which God gives to His children because of the sacrifice, death and resurrection of God's Son Jesus. You girls have been given all those gifts along with hope for the future. With what you've experienced, I think God will use you in helping others find out about Him."

Hana said, "Sara, you and Nyala have done so much for us. I'm sure I can speak for Lola and Maya and say we'll do all we can to serve Him while we serve others. Today wouldn't have happened without both of you."

Then Maya said, "Amen. I agree. The only sadness I feel today is for the other three girls we started this journey with four years ago. I wonder what's happened to Mariam, Makda and Zoya?"

Nyala asked, "Where are they?"

Maya answered, "Mariam was going to Dire Dawa to be a nanny. Makda was leaving for Saudi Arabia as a domestic worker and Zoya was a photography model. I hope they didn't experience any of the ugly stuff we have."

Lola said, "I never thought I'd be with the two of you again. Maybe someday we'll be able to see Mariam, Makda and Zoya."

Hana interjected, "One thing I know. Makda did something really special for us when she gave us a Bible. Over these last years, I don't know what I'd have done without the verses she taught us. I've thought about that and it reminded me of something.

"I lived in the south and most of the year it was dry, but we had a small plant growing there which my mom would use to make medicine. She'd gather the leaves and roots, boil them and give the medicine to us when we were sick and had a fever. I really hated the taste and smell of the medicine, but it worked.

"The plants which mom didn't gather would eventually bloom and release their seeds into the wind. A breeze would carry them away like a feather in every direction. When the seed landed, a new plant would grow and once again help others.

"It seems to me the plant was like the Bible. It had qualities that could heal if you used it. Then it would multiply and spread those qualities wherever God wanted it to go.

"Just listening to our stories makes me wonder how God is using each of us. We're like those fluffy and blowing seeds in the wind."

Maya, holding little Lola Marie, looked at Hana and Lola, and said, "I'm sure Mariam, Makda and Zoya are blooming wherever they are. Who knows, maybe someday we'll be sitting in six chairs sharing our 'seeds in the wind' stories with them!"

Lola Marie scooted off of Maya's lap and began playing with a cardboard box and some discarded wrapping paper.

For the first time in four years Maya felt hope. She felt peace. She felt real freedom.

Her thought was disrupted by a gentle kick from the new life within her.

Epilogue

Riyadh, Saudi Arabia – September 12, 2020

MAKDA

THE scream was out of her mouth before she could stop it! She quickly stepped back from the slanted window in front of her. They were almost 1,000 feet above the Riyadh, Saudi Arabian streets far below.

Hija sternly said, "Asad, an eleven-year-old Saudi boy knows better than that! It wasn't nice scaring Makda."

Asad hung his head in mock shame. Makda noticed his smile and laughed. "It's okay. I just wasn't quite ready for his push. I don't like high places!"

The Saudi family had decided to do some sightseeing in downtown Riyadh. Ammar, as an architect, had spent considerable time helping to design this particular building called *The Kingdom Centre*. He'd told Makda earlier that his area of expertise was designing the 'cores' which were supporting the massive building.

The family had taken an elevator to the 77th floor where they had visited the King Abdullah Mosque. Another elevator then took them to the 99th floor. There, they entered an enclosed skywalk suspended between the tops of two massive vertical towers that went upward from the main building. The skywalk had slanted glass windows stretching from floor to ceiling on both sides. As Makda had leaned over to look down, Asad hadn't been able to resist the scream-inducing nudge.

The family had grown to love Makda in the five years she'd been with them. The family's two girls were rapidly growing up. Esraa was now thirteen and Haifa was seven.

Ammar and Hija had accepted Makda into their family as a domestic worker and nanny. But, she'd become much more than that. Even though she was a Christian in a devout Muslim nation, there hadn't been any issues. Her faith was still intact and her daily focus was to make sure she never gave anyone any reason to think negatively about her Christianity.

Makda lingered at the window as the family moved further down the skywalk.

Looking at the horizon, she missed Ethiopia. Somewhere out there were her friends and family. Though she was loved by her Saudi family and she loved them, a part of her wondered if she'd ever see her five friends again. What had become of Mariam, Maya, Lola, Zoya and Hana?

Startled as someone touched her hand, she looked down at Haifa. The dark eyes and smile brushed away the momentary melancholy. Haifa said, "C'mon, it's time to go. We're stopping at the shopping mall on one of the lower floors. Papa said we're getting ice cream!"

Hand in hand, the two walked toward the rest of the family.

Abyei, Sudan – September 12, 2020

ZOYA

"**ANGEL** is a strange name for a boy."

Zoya looked at Jiri, the young woman who'd made the remark. Jiri's tendency to be straight forward and demeaning at times grated on her nerves. But Zoya was committed to showing love and patience to everyone in spite of the fact it was difficult at times. Her Christian faith commanded her to love everyone.

"I suppose the name seems odd to those who don't know the reason for it."

"Are you going to leave me hanging and not tell me the reason?"

Zoya asked, "Do you know what an angel is?"

"Of course. God has millions of them in Heaven."

"What are they like?"

Jiri responded, "They're beautiful, strong, busy and they fly."

Smiling, Zoya said, "You've known Angel for four years. Tell me what you see."

Jiri smiled and said, "Ah, I get it! He's a beautiful boy who thinks he's strong. And he's definitely busy because he always seems to be flying around the room."

"Well, there you have it. You've answered your own question about why I named him Angel."

Hesitating, Zoya wondered if she should go further. Then she said, "There's another reason I named him Angel."

Looking at the four-year-old playing with a game on the floor, Zoya said, "My memories of my father are very special. He called me Angel from as far back as I can remember. He never had to tell me he loved me because I could feel it every time he called me that special name. Naming my son Angel reminds me every day of my dad and mom. I don't want to forget them. They live on in my mind through Angel."

Jiri, for the first time Zoya could recall, had tear-filled eyes. "I didn't have a dad like that at all. In fact, I want to forget everything about him."

"You know what I think Jiri? I think you've resisted getting to know my God because of your relationship with your dad. My Father God isn't like your dad. My God loves unconditionally because He has perfect love. In fact the Bible says that He is love."

Jiri wiped her eyes and said, "Maybe you're right. My idea of who God is probably isn't right."

As Angel climbed onto Zoya's lap, her mind wondered... *'My life hadn't been easy, but I thank God for Angel. Being able to help Jiri and others know about God has to be the best job in the world.'*

Hugging Angel, Zoya smiled as she pressed her cheek against his.